The *W*ool Embroidery *Collection*

Gail Rogers

SALLYMILNER
PUBLISHING

To my mother and father, Meryll and Vern

To a very special mother, who is in her 90th year as this book goes to print, and my much loved father, who will sadly not be here to celebrate this book as he did my last with much pride.

First published in 2004 by

Sally Milner Publishing Pty Ltd

PO Box 2104

Bowral NSW 2576

Australia

© Gail Rogers

Design and page layout by Caroline Verity

Photography by Tim Connolly

Illustrations by Nicole Moffat

Edited by Kathryn Lamberton, Bridging the Gap, Sydney

Proofreading by Anne Rogers

Printed in China

National Library of Australia

Cataloguing-in-Publication data

Rogers, Gail.

Wool embroidery collection.

ISBN 1 86351 334 5.

1. Embroidery - Patterns. 2. Woolen goods. I. Title.
(Series : Milner craft series).

746.44041

10 9 8 7 6 5 4 3 2 1

DISCLAIMER

The information in this instruction book is presented in good faith. However, no warranty is given, nor results guaranteed, nor is freedom from any patent to be inferred. Since we have no control over the use of information contained in this book, the publisher and the author disclaim liability for untoward results.

Contents

Acknowledgements

How can you thank all the people who cross your path, inspire you and make you believe in yourself? Thank you one and all.

Like many, I have a very special family, a wonderful long-suffering husband and three of God's greatest gifts, my children. I wish to thank them so much for the greatest gift of all, their love and support.

Anne Rogers, hugs and thanks for being the sister I always wanted — you not only proofread this book and have such faith in what I do, but you also encouraged me to reach for the stars.

Special thanks to my extra special staff and teachers and to all the wonderful students and customers who have made the Kindred Spirits embroidery studio such a special place to be. The encouragement you have given me is second to none and much appreciated. Nicole Moffat, my special young friend, for being an extension of my arm and drawing my designs so beautifully, knowing exactly what I wanted. Pat O'Donnell, thank you for keeping me sane by constructing the dressing gown for me when I was on the last leg of the finishing touches for this book.

To my very special parents a thank you for giving me a wonderful start to a charmed life. And to Sally Milner Publishing for giving me the opportunity to produce my second book.

Ideas & Inspiration

*Flowers leave some of their fragrance
in the hand that bestows them.*
Chinese proverb

Where does it come from, this thing called inspiration?

All of us have different things that trigger an idea: a beautiful sunset for poetry, trickling rivers for dance, the sound of the wind in the trees for song — the list is endless. And for embroidery it is no different. Anyone who is drawn to make something with their hands feeds off what is happening around them. Every day wonderful things happen in this world of ours: an ant carrying a grain of sugar, puppies running like the wind just because they can, birds having a bath with total faith that they are safe. To live is to be inspired.

Ideas come from sight, sound, smell and touch: the sheen on an insect's wing, the softness of a baby's skin, the smell and shape of a flower bud opening to maturity — all of these things trigger inspiration.

I am constantly excited by all the remarkable songs, paintings, sculptures, music, art, poetry and novels that are provided for us to enjoy. A beautiful work of embroidery also excites the viewer.
If you love what you do you will be inspired. I love what I do, and to find enough time to stitch the ideas that are screaming around in my head is a constant struggle.

To try is to succeed; not to try is to mark time.

Introduction

ith exotic Colour Streams' silks, opulent Sheep's Silk and the truly beautiful Australian colours of Gumnut wools, this book provides an adventure into the wonderful world of wool embroidery. In many designs the embroidered wool is enhanced by the sparkle of Kreinik, the sheen of silk ribbon and the extra dimension of beads.

Teddy bears are particularly enjoyable to stitch, as you can spin a happy tale about what they are up to in the garden. I have used the same five playful bears with their different personalities for each of the blanket designs. These lively wee bears will create endless tales as you retell their stories to the very special little ones in your life. What a way to drift off to sleep, dreaming about mischievous bears having wonderful adventures in an enchanted garden. I have included stories with the designs: these might be the launch pad for your own, more detailed sagas.

The beautiful colours and shapes of Australian wildflowers come alive in the embroidered samplers. Australian wildflowers are some of the most exotic flowers to stitch, with colours as vibrant as Australia itself and magnificent forms, ranging from the Illyarrie (Eucalyptus erythrocorys) to the handsome flat pea (Platylobium formosum). Come for an Australian wildflower walk by creating your own sampler, or by stitching a single flower from these beautiful designs.

I have taken artistic licence in embellishing the colour and design of the flowers. The flowers are not to scale but are designed and stitched to give maximum impact.

The diversity of designs and projects in this book provides something for everyone. There is an embroidered woollen vest embellished with beads, a footstool highlighted with metallic threads, a blanket with geese strolling under a sparkling swag of beautiful ribbons, and an exotic crewel bell pull stitched in opulent silk and wool threads. As you absorb the designs presented, imagine them stitched on a variety of items — on clothing, table linen, wall hangings and bags, as well as on the items suggested at the beginning of each project.

Wool embroidery is an excellent technique for the novice embroiderer as it is such a forgiving medium. Wool blanketing, wool flannel and cashmere now come in a vast range of colours; not so long ago we could have any colour in wool as long as it was white! When I first started to create my own embroidery designs, the wool embroidery threads available were very limited, but today we have an excess of beautiful threads in wool, mohair, silk, rayon and cotton, all with choices of over-dyed and with very extensive colour ranges to choose from.

Anything goes in wool embroidery. If you think it is a good idea, it is a good idea. We are only limited in what we stitch by how far we push the boundaries of our creativity, as wool embroidery is an excellent medium to experiment with. I hope you enjoy your journey in wool embroidery as much as I have enjoyed putting it together. Knowing when to stop is my main problem; when I start stitching, it is so pleasurable that I have trouble putting my work down.

Many different designs are included in this book, from the beginner's level to the more advanced. I like to experiment with colour and to introduce metallic threads, beads, ribbons and any other embellishments that come to hand, so these have been included in some of the designs.

When designing something for the children in your life create an adventure in your mind so that you have a tale to tell to the lucky child. Nothing is better for a child than having their very own story that has been created especially for them.

Wool blankets are not only for babies today, but for adults as well — mother, father, brother, sister or best friend. To curl up with a good book or to watch a favourite television program wrapped in a gift that has been stitched by a friend or relative is to be wrapped in love. What shows love as much as a gift made with love? Maybe it is time to direct a little love to yourself as well.

I do hope you enjoy stitching these designs as much as I have enjoyed creating them. To be inspired is to inspire.

Happy stitching! *Gail Rogers*

Flora Abunda (1)
Australian wildflower sampler

This is the first of the wildflower blankets I designed and what fun it was. It is a very large project to stitch so make sure you set aside plenty of time. The flowers can be stitched and completed one at a time so that you feel a sense of achievement as you finish each flower. They can also be stitched individually for separate projects, as well as reduced in size to give the designs more applications.

If you would like to stitch any of these designs in silk on a finer fabric, Gumnut yarns have many of the same colours in silk threads, or at least a close colour match to the wool threads.

The designs can be stitched around the edge of a tablecloth, on the corners of napkins or on placemats. They would also enhance hot water bottle covers and hand towels to send overseas to friends and relatives. For the quilters among you, these designs would look wonderful set into a patchwork quilt.

THREADS

Gumnut Yarns Blossoms

038	645
077	646
116	648
118	679
193	708
275	746
277	748
349	829
367	859
549	869
554	949
567	963
589	987
597	990
608	991
628	994
629	999
643	

Gumnut Yarns Gemstones

AP3	G5
AP5	GL5
AZ4	H5
AZ5	TP4
B5	TP5
C5	Z4
G2	Z5

Anchor Marlitt

820	869
822	895
827	1003
838	1071
850	1209

DMC Rayon

30310	30712
30321	30745
30349	30818
30367	30895
30434	30915
30469	30976
30498	33820
30503	

REQUIREMENTS

Bottle green wool blanketing, 1.1m x 80cm (43" x 31 1/4")

Tartan of your choice, 1.3m x 1m (50 3/4" x 39")

Yellow piping, 4m (13')

Chenille needles, Nos 22, 24 (wool thread)

Crewel needles, No. 6 (wool thread), No. 9 (rayon thread)

Bottle green sewing thread to match wool blanketing

STITCHES

Back stitch	Satin stitch
Bullion stitch	Padded satin stitch
Chain stitch	Slanted satin stitch
Whipped chain stitch	Sloping satin stitch
Colonial knot	Stem stitch
Fly stitch	Whipped stem stitch
French knot	Straight stitch
Lazy daisy	Tacking stitch
Pistil stitch	

PREPARATION

Stitch a tacking stitch 5cm (2") in from the top, sides and bottom of the blanket — this gives you the guide line for the piping and for the backing fabric fold-over. Fold the blanket in half horizontally, run a large tacking thread down the middle fold, and then fold in half vertically and tack down this line to give you the centre of the blanket. With a tacking stitch, divide the blanket into 16 equal rectangles, each 25cm (9 3/4") high x 17.5cm (6 7/8") wide

Marking the design on the blanket is quite difficult when using wool blanketing. One method is to trace the design onto paper, and then pin the paper to the fabric and outline the design using running stitches by hand or machine. As a general guide for the embroidery, I use a blue water-erasable pen to mark the main lines and then embroider the design freehand. Another method is to trace the design onto water-soluble Vilene and then tack that to the blanket. If you are using a pale fabric, trace the design onto tracing paper and then pin the paper in place. Make holes in the tracing paper with an awl or knitting needle and, with a water-soluble marking pen, mark dots on the blanket where you want to place the flowers. If using any other fabric, pin the design under the fabric and hold it up to a window, or use a light box, to trace the design onto the fabric. Whichever method you choose will require patience but the results are worthwhile.

EMBROIDERY INSTRUCTIONS

All embroidery is worked with a single strand unless otherwise stated. The illustrations are reduced, and must be enlarged to be worked on at original size. Please check instuctions with each design.

With this design, as with all embroidery, I have taken artistic licence in embellishing the colour and design of the flowers. The flowers are not to scale but were designed and stitched to give maximum impact.

Illustrations for these flowers should be enlarged. An enlargement guide for photocopying is on page 174.

CONSTRUCTION OF THE FINISHED BLANKET

Cut your backing fabric 1.3m x 1m (50 3/4" x 39"). This will leave a 10cm (4") overhang on all sides of your blanket when the two are pinned together. Pin the piping 5cm (2") from the edge of the blanket, raw edges to the outside. Cut and overlap the corners, and pin and stitch in place using a zipper foot (Fig. 1). Place the backing fabric face down on a table, then place the embroidered blanket right side up on top and pin in place. Fold the corners over, the same way you would if you were covering a book, at a 45° angle (Fig. 2). Fold the sides over and turn under 5cm (2"), then turn over again so that you have a 5cm (2") double thickness border on the front of the blanket. Pin in place. Trim away any material showing at the corners so that there is a mitred edge. Hand-stitch the backing in place (Fig. 3).

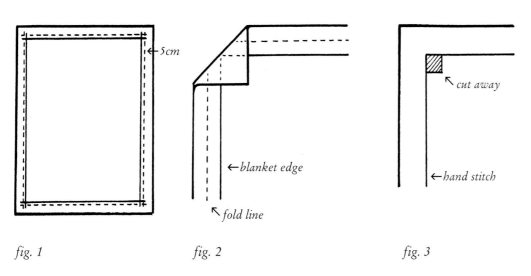

fig. 1   *fig. 2*   *fig. 3*

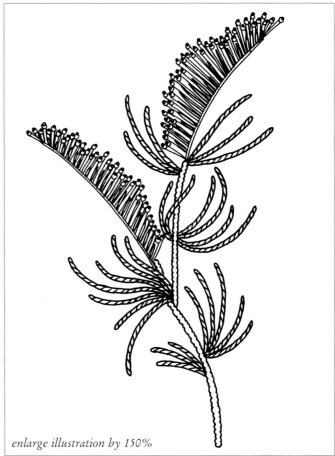

enlarge illustration by 150%

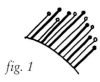

fig. 1

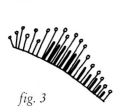

fig. 2

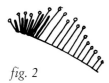

fig. 3

Flame Grevillea (*Grevillea eriostachya*)

Threads
Blossoms, 608, 708, 746
Gemstones, G2
DMC Rayon, 33820, 30503
Marlitt, 850

Stems Stitch the stem in whipped chain stitch with Gemstones G2.

Flowers Stitch the stamens in uneven pistil stitches in Blossoms 746 and Blossoms 708, alternating the colours to create shading (Fig. 1). Stem stitch the backbone of the flower head in Blossoms 746. With DMC 33820 stitch French knots at the tips of the stamens (Fig. 2). Work straight stitches between the stamens at the top section of the flowers in DMC 30503, then add straight stitches between the rest of the stamens in Marlitt 850 (Figs 2 & 3).

Leaves Stem stitch the leaves using Blossoms 608.

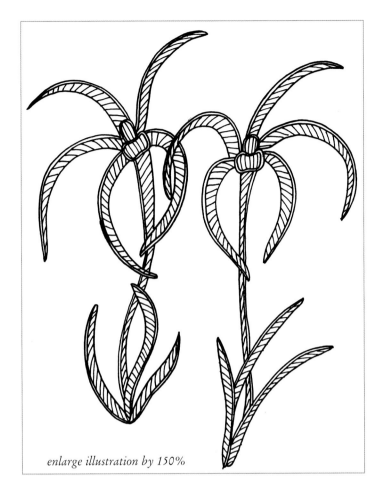

enlarge illustration by 150%

Common Spider Orchid (*Caladenia patersonii*)

Threads

Blossoms, 991

Gemstones, GL5, C5

DMC Rayon, 30469

Flowers Stitch the petals and the centre labellum in satin stitch with Blossoms 991, then stem stitch down one side and around the labellum in Gemstones GL5 (Fig. 1). Stitch the column in satin stitch with Gemstones C5, then stem stitch around the outside of the column in the same colour (Fig. 2).

Stems and leaves Stitch the stems and leaves in a slanted satin stitch with Gemstones C5. Highlight down one side of the leaves and stem with stem stitch, using DMC 30469 (Fig. 3).

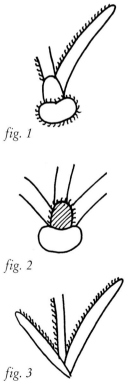

fig. 1

fig. 2

fig. 3

enlarge illustration by 150%

fig. 1

fig. 2

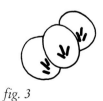

fig. 3

fig. 4

Sturts Desert Pea (*Clianthus formosus*)

Threads

Blossoms, 829, 990, 999

Gemstones, G5

DMC Rayon, 30349, 30310

Flowers Stitch the petals with slanted satin stitch in Blossoms 829 (Fig. 1). Stitch around the outside edge of each petal in stem stitch with DMC 30349, then add a single straight stitch in Blossoms 999, coming up at the base and going down half-way up the centre petal (Fig. 1). Fill in the centres of the flowers with satin stitch in Blossoms 999 and then, with DMC 30310, highlight around the outside edge of the centres with small straight stitches. Add some straight stitch highlights at the top and bottom of the centres in the same colour (Fig. 2). For the white highlights stitch small uneven straight stitches in the centre with Blossoms 990 (Fig. 3).

Buds Stitch the petals with slanted satin stitch in Blossoms 829. Stem stitch around the outside edge of each petal in DMC 30349.

Stems and leaves Stem stitch the stems with Gemstones G5. Stitch 2 lazy daisy stitches at the top of each bud, then finish with a French knot in the same colour (Fig. 4). Stitch the leaves in satin stitch with Gemstones G5.

enlarge illustration by 150%

Blue Lechenaultia (Lechenaultia biloba)

Threads

Blossoms, 987, 990, 994

Gemstones, AZ4, AZ5, B5, TP4

DMC Rayon, 30895

Flowers Stitch the petals in slanted satin stitch, using Gemstones AZ5 for some flowers and Gemstones AZ4 for the rest, to create shading (Fig. 1). For the centres, stitch uneven straight stitches in Blossoms 990 (Fig. 2). Finish with a single French knot in Gemstones TP4 for the centre.

Stems Chain stitch the main stems with Blossoms 994. Stitch the stems for the leaves in stem stitch with Blossoms 987.

Leaves With Gemstones B5 and DMC 30895 threaded together in the needle, stitch small straight stitches for the leaves.

fig. 1

fig. 2

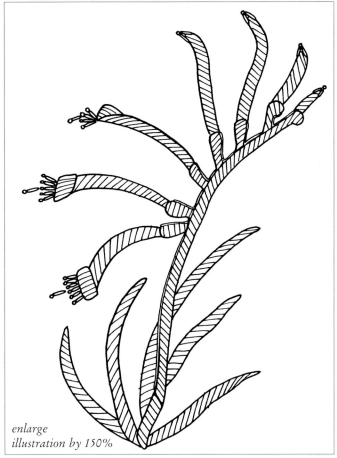

enlarge illustration by 150%

fig. 1

fig. 2

fig. 3

fig. 4

Mangles Kangaroo Paw (*Anigozanthos manglesii*)

Threads

Blossoms, 038, 629
Gemstones, TP4, Z4
DMC Rayon, 30321, 30895

Stem Stitch the stem with satin stitch in Blossoms 038, then highlight down one side with stem stitch in DMC 30321. (Fig. 1).

Flowers Satin stitch the petals with Blossoms 629. At the tip of the top 4 petals stitch 2 straight stitch highlights forming an inverted V with Blossoms 038, then stitch a French knot at the tip of the V with DMC 30321 (Fig. 2). On the 3 lower petals satin stitch the lobes in Gemstones TP4, use straight stitch in Gemstones Z4 for the whiskers (Fig. 3), then stitch French knots in DMC 30321 at the tips of the whiskers. Finish with a pistil stitch tongue in DMC 30895 (Fig. 4).

Leaves Stitch the leaves in slanted satin stitch with Blossoms 629.

enlarge illustration by 150%

Pink Star Flower (*Calytrix bevifolia*)

Threads Blossoms, 077, 589, 708; Gemstones, H5;
DMC Rayon, 30915; Marlitt, 822, 1209

Flowers Stitch the petals with satin stitch in Blossoms 077 (Fig. 1). Work the stamens in uneven straight stitch radiating out from the centre of the flower in Blossoms 708 (Fig. 2). Highlight the tips of the stamens and centre of the flower with French knots in Marlitt 822. Highlight the tips of the petals in DMC 30915 with a fly stitch and a small straight stitch tail (Fig. 3). Stitch the tendrils in Marlitt 1209 with a very tiny stem stitch.

Buds Stitch the buds with satin stitch in Blossoms 077 (see Fig. 1 above). Highlight the tips of the petals in DMC 30915 with a fly stitch and a small straight stitch tail (see Fig. 3 above). With Gemstones H5 stitch 4 straight stitches, going in and out of the same hole and making sure to lay the thread to the left of the centre stitch, then to the right of the centre stitch. Finish with another centre stitch (Fig. 4). Repeat for the other side of the bud. To finish the bud, stitch 4 straight stitches in Gemstones H5 at the base of the bud (Fig. 5).

Stems Stitch the stems in chain stitch with Gemstones H5. The seed pods on the stems are stitched in the same thread, with 6 straight stitches going in and out of the same hole. Be sure to lay the thread to the left and right of the centre stitch (see Fig. 4 above).

Leaves The leaves are stitched with 10- to 12-wrap bullions in Blossoms 589.

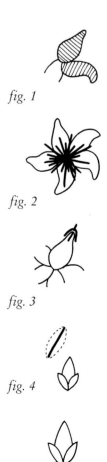

fig. 1

fig. 2

fig. 3

fig. 4

fig. 5

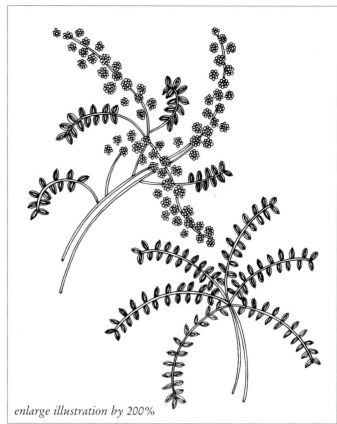

enlarge illustration by 200%

Sunshine Wattle (*Acacia terminalis*)

Threads

Blossoms, 549, 708, 987

Marlitt, 820

Blossom Stitch the blossoms, using Blossoms 708, in French knots placed very close together. To create the raised effect, stitch more French knots on top of the first layer of the blossom. Highlight the blossoms with Marlitt 820 by stitching 4–6 French knots on top of each of the blossoms.

Stems Work the stems in stem stitch with Blossoms 987.

Leaves The leaves are stitched in lazy daisy stitch with a straight stitch placed in the middle of each lazy daisy stitch, using Blossoms 549 (Fig. 1).

fig. 1

enlarge illustration by 150%

Wedding Bush (*Ricinocarpos pinifolius*)

Threads

Blossoms, 643, 648, 679, 748, 859, 990

Marlitt, 895

Flowers Fill the petals in with satin stitch in Blossoms 990. To create the shadow radiating out from the centre of the petals stitch 3 straight stitches in Blossoms 643 (Fig. 1). Stitch French knots for the centre of the flowers in Blossoms 748. For the highlights, stem stitch around the outside of each petal in Marlitt 895, then stitch 2 straight stitch highlights coming out from the centre of each petal between the shadow highlights (Fig. 2). Stitch the base of the small flowers in satin stitch with Blossoms 679.

Seed pods Stitch the base of the pods in satin stitch with Blossoms 679 and stitch 6 vertical straight stitches across the top of the bud in the same colour (Fig. 3). Stitch French knots at the top of the bud in Blossoms 859 and highlight the bud between the base and the 6 vertical stitches in the same colour, using a single straight stitch in Blossoms 859 (Fig. 4).

Stems Chain stitch the stems in Blossoms 648.

Leaves Stitch a double row of stem stitch side by side for the leaves in Blossoms 679, making one side shorter than the other.

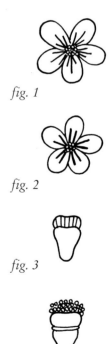

fig. 1

fig. 2

fig. 3

fig. 4

enlarge illustration by 150%

fig. 1

fig. 2

fig. 3

fig. 4

fig. 5

Yellow Guinea Flower (*Hibbertia serpyllifolia*)

Threads

Blossoms, 567, 708, 869; Gemstones, H5, TP5;
DMC Rayon, 30367, 30498, 33820

Flowers Stitch the petals in blanket stitch with Blossoms 708 (Fig. 1). Highlight the centres of the flowers in Gemstones TP5 with straight stitches radiating out from the centre of the flower (Fig. 2). Stitch the centre with DMC 33820 in satin stitch. Stitch highlights on the outside edges of the petals in straight stitch angled into the centre in the same colour (Fig. 3).

Buds Stitch the base of the buds in satin stitch with Blossoms 708. Satin stitch the top of the bud in Gemstones H5, overlapping the base. Highlight the tip of the bud with 2 fly stitches in DMC 30498. Finish by putting a fly stitch around the tip of the bud and 1 small straight stitch coming up at the tip of the bud and going down in the centre of the bud, using the same colour (Fig. 4).

Stems Chain stitch the stems in Blossoms 869.

Leaves Fill the leaves in with 3 straight stitches in Blossoms 567, going in and out of the same hole and laying the thread to the left, then to the right of the centre stitch (Fig. 5). Stitch highlights around each leaf with a lazy daisy stitch in DMC 30367.

enlarge illustration by 150%

Blue Finger Flower (*Cheiranthera linearis*)

Threads

Blossoms, 349, 367, 589, 748, 949

Marlitt, 838

Flowers The petals of the flowers are stitched in Blossoms 367. Stitch a large lazy daisy stitch for each petal, then fill in the lazy daisy stitch with 6 to 8 straight stitches to give the petals a padded look (Fig. 1). With Marlitt 838 stitch a fly stitch around the tip of each petal, then stitch straight stitch highlights at the base and tip of the petals (Fig. 2). Stitch a lazy daisy stitch between each petal in Blossoms 349 (Fig. 3). Stitch 4 French knots to fill in the centre with Blossoms 589. For the stamens stitch 5 bullions of 5 to 7 wraps each radiating out from the centre of the flower, in Blossoms 748 (Fig. 4).

Stems Chain stitch the stems in Blossoms 949.

Leaves Stem stitch the leaves in Blossoms 589.

fig. 1

fig. 2

fig. 3

fig. 4

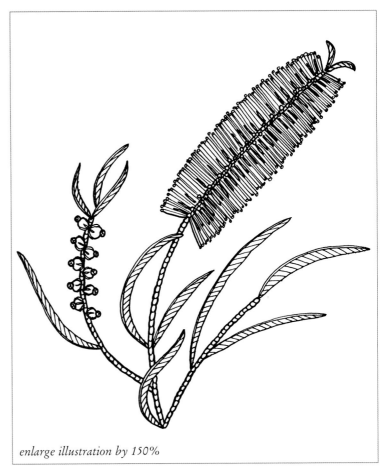

enlarge illustration by 150%

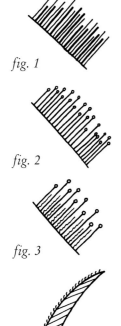

fig. 1

fig. 2

fig. 3

fig. 4

fig. 5

Weeping Bottle Brush (*Callistemon viminalis*)

Threads Blossoms, 629, 645, 829, 859, 963; Gemstones, AP3, AP5 Marlitt, 827, 869, 1003, 1071

Stems Chain stitch the stems in Gemstones AP5, stitching right to the tip of the flower head.

Flower Stitch uneven straight stitch petals, alternating Blossoms 829 and Blossoms 859 (Fig. 1). On the tips of the petals stitch the anthers with Marlitt 869 in French knots (Fig. 2). With Marlitt 827 stitch uneven highlights between each petal in straight stitch, starting at the centre of the flower and going down half-way along the petals (Fig. 3).

Centres With Blossoms 645 stitch French knots along the stem of the flower head.

Leaves Stitch the leaves with slanted satin stitch in Blossoms 629. Highlight the leaves by adding stem stitch in Marlitt 1071 along the upper side of the leaf (Fig. 4).

Nut seed pods Stitch the seed pods using 6 to 7 satin stitches in Gemstones AP3 and stitch a French knot at the tip of the pod in Blossoms 963. Highlight the pods with Marlitt 1003 by stitching a fly stitch around the pod, then stitching a straight stitch that comes up at the base of the pod and goes down in the centre of the pod (Fig. 5).

Swan River Daisy (*Brachycome iberidifolia*)

Threads

Blossoms, 275, 277, 597, 648, 748

DMC Rayon, 30434

Marlitt, 827

Flowers Satin stitch the petals of the flowers with Blossoms 277 (marked A on the design) and Blossoms 275 (marked B on the design). Fill in the centres with French knots in Blossoms 748 and DMC 30434 threaded in the same needle. Stitch extra French knots in between the existing French knots with Blossoms 648 and Marlitt 827 threaded in the same needle.

Stems and leaves Stitch the stems in whipped stem stitch with Blossoms 597, then stitch irregular shaped fly stitches in the same colour for the leaves (Fig. 1).

fig. 1

enlarge illustration by 150%

fig. 1

fig. 2

fig. 3

Geraldton Wax (*Chamelaucium uncinatum*)

Threads
Blossoms, 116, 118, 193, 628
Gemstones, Z5
DMC Rayon, 30818

Stems Stem stitch the stems with Gemstones Z5.

Flowers Fill in each petal with a padded satin stitch in Blossoms 116. Fill in the centre of the flowers with padded satin stitch in Blossoms 118. Highlight around the centres of the flowers by stitching small back stitches in Blossoms 193 and DMC 30818 threaded in the same needle (Fig. 1).

Buds Fill in the bud with padded satin stitch in Gumnut Blossoms 118, then stitch 2 small straight stitches on each side of the base of the bud in Blossoms 628 (Fig. 2).

Leaves Fill in the leaves with slanted satin stitch in Blossoms 628 (Fig. 3).

enlarge illustration by 150%

Flannel Flower (*Actinotus helianthi*)

Threads

Blossoms, 554, 991

Gemstones, G2

DMC Rayon, 30712

Petals Fill in the petals with satin stitch in Blossoms 991 (Fig. 1). Fill in the centres with French knots in Blossoms 554 and DMC 30712, threaded together in the same needle. Again with Blossoms 554 and DMC 30712, stitch a fly stitch around the tip of each petal. Using the same thread, finish with a straight stitch, starting at the tip of the petal and going down half-way along the petal (Fig. 2).

Buds Stitch the buds in the same manner as the petals, but add small straight stitches at the base of the buds in Gemstones G2 (Fig. 3).

Stems and leaves With Gemstones G2 stem stitch the stems, fly stitch the leaves in the same colour, and then add a small straight stitch at the tip of each leaf again in the same colour. With Gemstones G2 stitch some lazy daisy stitches along the stems (Fig. 4).

Small flower pods With Gemstones G2, stitch the small flower pods in colonial knots and the stems in straight stitches (Fig. 5).

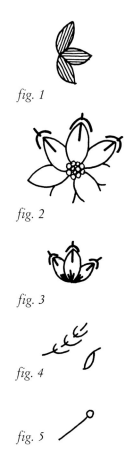

fig. 1

fig. 2

fig. 3

fig. 4

fig. 5

enlarge illustration by 150%

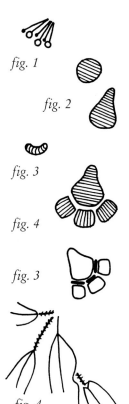

fig. 1

fig. 2

fig. 3

fig. 4

fig. 3

fig. 4

Illyarrie (*Eucalyptus erythrocorys*)

Threads

Blossoms, 628, 629, 746, 829, 949

DMC Rayon, 33820

Flower Stitch uneven pistil stitches for the filaments in Blossoms 746, then with DMC 33820 stitch in between each filament with pistil stitches (Fig. 1). Fill in the centre of the open flower and the receptacle of the half-open flower with satin stitch in Blossoms 628 (Fig. 2). Finish the centre of the open flower with 1 bullion stitch of 12 wraps in Blossoms 746 (Fig. 3).

Buds Satin stitch the caps on the buds in Blossoms 829, then satin stitch the receptacle of the buds in Blossoms 628 (Fig. 4). To finish, add a straight stitch between each cap and the receptacle in Blossoms 746 (Fig. 5).

Leaves Stitch the leaves in a slanted satin stitch in Blossoms 629.

Stems Stitch the stems in chain stitch with Blossoms 949. Join the leaves to the stems with stem stitch in the same colour, then whip with Blossoms 829 through the stem stitch (Fig. 6).

enlarge illustration by 150%

Scented Sun Orchid (*Thelymitra ixioides*)

Threads

Blossoms, 645, 646, 748, 990

Gemstones, AZ4

DMC Rayon, 30469, 30976

fig. 1

Flowers Satin stitch the petals in Gemstones AZ4 (Fig. 1). Stitch small straight stitches between each petal in Blossoms 990, then using the same colour stitch a 10-wrap bullion in the centre of the flower, creating a loop (Fig. 2). Hold this loop down with a small straight stitch. Finish with a single French knot, using Blossoms 748 and DMC 30976 threaded together in the same needle. Stitch the base of the flowers in satin stitch with Blossoms 645, then stitch a fly stitch around the base in DMC 30469 (Fig. 3).

fig. 2

Buds Satin stitch the buds in Gemstones AZ4, then stitch the base of the buds in satin stitch with Blossoms 645. Stitch a fly stitch around the base in DMC 30469 (see Fig. 3 above).

fig. 3

Stems Chain stitch the stems in Blossoms 645.

Leaves Stitch the leaves with a slanted satin stitch in Blossoms 646 and highlight the outside edge of the leaves in stem stitch with DMC 30469 (Fig. 4).

Flora Abunda (2)
Australian wildflower sampler

A range of beautiful Australian wildflowers which are stitched in exotic Australian hand-dyed wools on rich Australian wool blanketing. I had a wonderful time creating this second blanket in my range of wildflower designs and didn't want to stop.

This blanketing is so nice to snuggle up under on those cold winter stitching days or when you watch television. Now is the time to stitch one for yourself and your partner, or your parents. The amount of work in this blanket is not for the beginner or the faint-hearted. You could stitch elements of the design in a mix and match format, or as a single design on its own. Enjoy stitching the flowers as much as I have, have fun and take time out to be creative.

THREADS

Gumnut Yarns Blossoms

039	637
059	648
074	679
093	708
099	728
213	748
215	787
297	827
299	849
386	851
387	859
540	943
549	947
577	949
606	963
607	967
608	983
616	985
628	990
636	

Gumnut Yarns Gemstones

AP3	E4
AP5	E5
AZ1	G5
AZ5	H4
C5	

DMC Rayon Floss

30300	30742
30301	30798
30322	30814
30336	30818
30349	30839
30367	30841
30415	30895
30434	30898
30469	30973
30472	30976
30498	30991
30501	33371
30510	33607
30552	33608
30580	33685
30581	33820
30676	35200

REQUIREMENTS

Tan wool blanketing, 1.1m x 80cm (43" x 31 1/4")

Matching plaid, 1.3m x 1m (50 3/4" x 39")

Maroon piping, 4m (13')

Chenille needles, Nos 22, 24 (wool thread)

Crewel needles, No. 6 (wool thread), No. 9 (rayon thread)

Tan sewing thread to match wool blanketing

STITCHES

Back stitch	*Lazy daisy stitch*
Blanket stitch	*Needle painting*
Bullion stitch	*Satin stitch*
Chain stitch	*Padded satin stitch*
Whipped chain	*Slanted satin stitch*
Colonial knot	*Split stitch*
Fly stitch	*Stem stitch*
French knot	*Straight stitch*

PREPARATION

Stitch a tacking stitch 5cm (2") in from the top, sides and bottom of the blanket — this gives you the guide line for the piping and for the backing fabric fold-over. Fold the blanket in half horizontally and run a large tacking thread down the middle fold. Next, fold in half vertically and tack down this line to give you the centre of the blanket. With a tacking stitch, divide the blanket into 16 equal rectangles, each 25cm (9 3/4") high x 20cm (8") wide.

Marking the design on the blanket is quite difficult when using wool blanketing. One method is to trace the design onto paper, and then pin the paper to the fabric and outline the design using running stitches by hand or machine. As a general guide for the embroidery, I use a blue water-erasable pen to mark the main lines and embroider the design freehand. Another method is to trace the design onto water-soluble Vilene, and then tack that to the blanket. If you are using a pale fabric, trace the design onto tracing paper, then pin the paper in place. Make holes in the tracing paper with an awl or knitting needle and, with a water-soluble marking pen, mark dots on the blanket where you want to place the flowers. If using any other fabric, pin the design under the fabric and hold it up to a window, or use a light box, and trace the design onto the fabric. Whichever method you choose will require patience, but the results are worthwhile.

EMBROIDERY INSTRUCTIONS

All embroidery is worked with a single strand unless otherwise stated. The illustrations are reduced, and must be enlarged to be worked on at original size. Please check instuctions with each design.

With this design, as with all embroidery, I have taken artistic licence in embellishing the colour and design of the flowers. The flowers are not to scale but were designed and stitched to give maximum impact.

Illustrations for these flowers should be enlarged. An enlargement guide for photocopying is on page 174.

CONSTRUCTION OF THE FINISHED BLANKET

Cut your backing fabric 1.3m x 1m (50 $^3/_4$" x 39"). This will leave a 10cm (4") overhang on all sides of your blanket when the two are pinned together. Pin the piping 5cm (2") from the edge of the blanket, raw edges to the outside. Cut and overlap the corners, and pin and stitch in place using a zipper foot (Fig. 1). Place the backing fabric face down on a table, then place the embroidered blanket right side up on top and pin in place. Fold the corners over, the same way you would if you were covering a book, at a 45° angle (Fig. 2). Fold the sides over and turn under 5cm (2"), then turn over again so that you have a 5cm (2") double thickness border on the front of the blanket. Pin in place. Trim away any material showing at the corners so that there is a mitred edge. Hand-stitch the backing in place (Fig. 3).

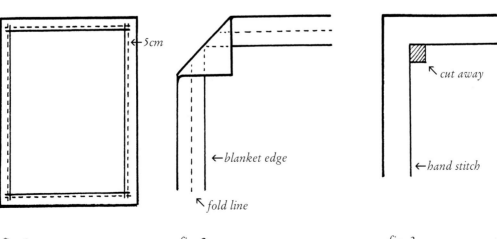

fig. 1   fig. 2   fig. 3

enlarge illustration by 150%

fig. 1

fig. 2

fig. 3a

fig. 3b

fig. 3c

Southern Cross (*Xanthosia rotundifolia*)

Threads Blossoms, 949, 990; Gemstones, E5
DMC Rayon Floss, 30434, 30472, 30676, 30814, 35200

Flowers Fill in the petals of the flowers with satin stitch using Blossoms 990. Stitch the flower stalk in Blossoms 990 with straight stitches, then highlight it with 3 straight stitches in DMC 30472 and DMC 30676 threaded together in the same needle (Fig. 1). Stitch fly stitch highlights at the tip of each petal in DMC 30814 (Fig. 1). Stitch the small flowerets scattered around the centre of the flower with 2 strands of DMC 35200, in a circle of 5 French knots. Stitch a single French knot in the middle of each floweret with 1 strand of DMC 30814.

Leaves Fill in the leaves in slanted satin stitch using Gemstones E5. Stem stitch highlights around each leaf in DMC 30434. Back stitch down the centre of each leaf in Blossoms 949, then stitch straight stitches in Blossoms 949 from each point of the leaf, going in at the vein (Fig. 2).

Stems Stitch the stems in Blossoms 949 in stem stitch, making the stitches longer and wider towards the bottom of the stem. Highlight one side of the stem in stem stitch with DMC 30434.

Buds Stitch 3 small straight stitches slanted downward in the middle of the bud in Blossoms 949 (Fig. 3a), then stitch 2 very small straight stitches at the tip of the bud in Gemstones E5 (Fig. 3b) and 2 straight stitches on either side of the bud in the same colour (Fig. 3c). All the stitches should face downward to the base of the bud.

enlarge illustration by 200%

Fairy Fan Flowers (*Scaevola aemula*)

Threads Blossoms, 213, 215, 606, 608, 609, 990
DMC Rayon Floss, 30839, 30973, 33607, 33608, 33685

Flowers Fill in the petals on the 4 dark flowers with straight stitches in Blossoms 215. Highlight the centre of each petal in 3 straight stitches with DMC 33685, then work a fly stitch around the outside of the petal in DMC 33607 (Fig. 1). Fill the centre of the flower with small straight stitches in Blossoms 990. Highlight the centre of this with small straight stitches in DMC 30973 (Fig. 2), then back stitch around the outside of the white section with DMC 30839 (Fig. 3).
Fill in the petals on the 2 pale flowers with straight stitches in Blossoms 213, highlight the centre of each petal with 3 straight stitches in DMC 33607, and then place a fly stitch around the outside of the petal in DMC 33608 (see Fig. 1 above). Fill the centre of the flower with small straight stitches in Blossoms 990. Highlight the centre of this with small straight stitches in DMC 30973 (see Fig. 2 above), then stitch around the outside of the white section in small back stitches with DMC 30839 (see Fig. 3 above).

Large leaves Fill in the leaves with slanted satin stitch, sloping towards the centre vein of the leaf, in Blossoms 608 and Blossoms 609. Alternate the colours for the leaves to create shading and depth. Stem stitch around the underside of the leaf and the vein in DMC 30839.

Small leaves Stitch the small leaves and the leaves around the flowers with 3 to 4 straight stitches, going in and out of the same hole to create small pointed leaves, in Blossoms 608 and Blossoms 606 (Fig. 4a). Stitch a fly stitch around each of these leaves in DMC 30839 (Fig. 4b).

Stems Stitch the stems in long stem stitch with Blossoms 608, making them thicker at the bottom. Highlight down one side of the stem in stem stitch with DMC 30839.

fig. 1

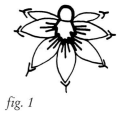

fig. 2

fig. 3

fig. 4a

fig. 4b

enlarge illustration by 200%

fig. 1

fig. 2

fig. 3

fig. 4

Swamp Donkey Orchid (*Diuris pauciflora*)

Threads

Blossoms, 708, 859

Gemstones, E4, E5

DMC Rayon Floss, 30427, 30472, 30498

Flowers and buds Fill the petals of the flowers in straight stitch with Blossoms 708, and then, with Blossoms 859, highlight the centre of the flowers with small straight stitches (Fig. 1). Stitch extra straight stitch highlights over the red highlights and on the upper petals in DMC 30498 (Fig. 2). Stitch two 10- to 12-wrap bullions coming out from the middle petal in DMC 30472 (Fig. 3). Work straight stitch highlights in Blossoms 859 and DMC 30498 for the buds and the heads of the flowers (Fig. 4).

Stems and leaves Stitch the stems with long stem stitch, laid side by side to create a thicker stem, in Gemstones E4 and Gemstones E5. Alternate the colours for the leaves and stems to create shading and depth. The leaves are worked with stem stitch, stitched closer together, in Gemstones E4 and Gemstones E5. Highlight the leaves and stems on one side in stem stitch with DMC 30427.

enlarge illustration by 200%

Gungurra (*Eucalyptus caesia*)

Threads Blossoms, 039, 099, 606, 607, 963
DMC Rayon Floss, 30349, 30469, 30814, 33820

Leaves and stems Stitch the leaves in slanted satin stitch, facing into the vein of the leaf, with Blossoms 607 and Blossoms 606. Alternate the colours for the leaves to create shading and depth. Stitch the stem and the upper two-thirds of the vein of the leaf in stem stitch in Blossoms 099 (Fig. 1), making the stem stitch wider and more like a slanted satin stitch where the leaf joins the stem, then stitch the last one-third at the tip of the vein in stem stitch with DMC 30814. Highlight the outside edge of the leaf and one side of the stem in DMC 30814 (Fig. 2).

Flowers Stitch uneven straight stitch stamens in Blossoms 039 and straight stitch highlights between the stamens in DMC 30349, and then stitch colonial knots at the tip of each stamen in DMC 33820 (Fig. 3).

Cap Stitch the hemispherical cap in straight stitches in Blossoms 963, then stitch over this again in the same colour to pad the cap. Highlight the cap with straight stitches in DMC 30814, which will create shadows and texture (Fig. 3).

Buds Stitch the top and bottom of the buds in the same manner and in the same colour as the caps. Highlight the top, centre and sides in DMC 30814 in uneven straight stitches (Fig. 4). Highlight the bottom of the bud with straight stitches in DMC 30469 (Fig. 5).

Stems For the stems, stitch 2 rows of stem stitch in Blossoms 963, then highlight down the centre of the stem in stem stitch with DMC 30814 (Fig. 6).

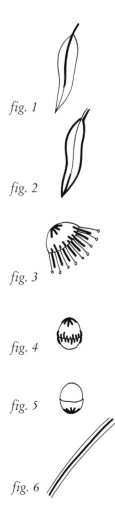

fig. 1

fig. 2

fig. 3

fig. 4

fig. 5

fig. 6

enlarge illustration by 150%

fig. 1

Cut-leaf Hibbertia (*Hibbertia cuneiformis*)

Threads Blossoms, 549, 708, 967
DMC Rayon Floss, 30841, 30973, 30976, 30991

Flowers Stitch the petals in long and short blanket stitch in Blossoms 708. Stitch the centre highlights with DMC 30976 in long and short straight stitches (Fig. 1). Highlight around the petals in stem stitch with DMC 30976 to create the shading (Fig. 1). Fill the centres with 13–16 bullions of 20–25 wraps each in DMC 30973, laying some bullions over each other.

Buds Stitch the buds in blanket stitch with Blossoms 708. Stitch the highlights with DMC 30976 in long and short straight stitches.

Seed pod Fill in the sepals with satin stitch in Blossoms 967. Fill in the centre with 10 French knots in Blossoms 967 and Blossoms 708 threaded together in the same needle. Stitch highlights around the outside of the pod in stem stitch with DMC 30841.

Stem The stems are stitched in chain stitch in Blossoms 967 and highlighted on one side with DMC 30841 in stem stitch.

Leaves Fill in the leaves with satin stitch in Blossoms 549, then stem stitch down the vein of the leaf in DMC 30991.

Buds Stitch 3–4 straight stitches on each side and in the middle of the large bud, in Blossoms 549. For the small bud stitch 2 small straight stitches on either side of the bud. Finish by using DMC 30991 to straight stitch highlights, close around the green.

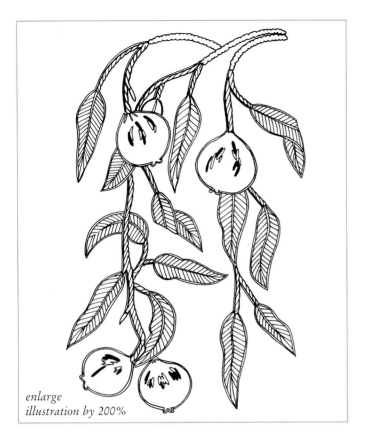

enlarge
illustration by 200%

Quandong (Native Peach) (*Santalum acuminatum*)

Threads

Blossoms, 607, 628, 679, 859, 949, 985, 990

DMC Rayon Floss, 30301, 30498, 30580, 30895

Fruit Fill in the fruit with needle painting in Blossoms 859. Leave small gaps, and in them stitch the highlights on the fruit with straight stitches, some in Blossoms 990 and the rest in Blossoms 679. Stitch around the outside of the fruit in stem stitch with DMC 30498.

Leaves Stitch the leaves in slanted satin stitch facing into the vein of each leaf. Use Blossoms 607 and Blossoms 628 alternately for the leaves, to create shading and depth. Stem stitch highlights around the outside edge and down the centre of each leaf — in DMC 30895 for the leaves stitched with Blossoms 628, and DMC 30580 for the leaves stitched with Blossoms 607.

Stems Stitch the stems with stem stitch in Blossoms 949 and highlight one side of each stem in stem stitch with DMC 30301. Work the old stem at the top of the design with a whipped chain stitch in Blossoms 985 and the 2 dead tips on the main branch with 2 small straight stitches in the same colour (Fig. 1).

fig. 1

enlarge illustration by 200%

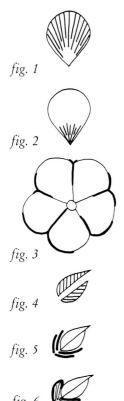

fig. 1

fig. 2

fig. 3

fig. 4

fig. 5

fig. 6

Rainbow Plant (*Byblis gigantea*)

Threads Blossoms, 297, 299, 616
DMC Rayon Floss, 30336, 30469, 33820

Flowers Fill in the outside of the petals with long and short straight stitch in Blossoms 297 (Fig. 1), then fill the centre of the flower with long and short straight stitches in Blossoms 299 (Fig. 2). Stitch 3, 25-wrap bullions, laid horizontally side by side across the centre of the flower, in DMC 33820. Stitch a 20-wrap vertical bullion, coming from the centre top of the bullions in DMC 33820, then stitch a yellow colonial knot in the same colour at the top of the white bullion. Highlight the shadows of the flower in DMC 30336, using stem stitch (Fig. 3).

Buds Fill in the upper side of the buds with satin stitch in Blossoms 297, then stitch the other side of the bud in Blossoms 299 (Fig. 4). Stitch 2 straight stitches on each side of the bud in Blossoms 616 (Fig. 5), then stitch 2 small fly stitches with long tails in DMC 30469 at the tip of the bud. Highlight the stamens cupping the bud in stem stitch in the same colour (Fig. 6).

Stems and leaves The stems and leaves are stitched with long stem stitch in Blossoms 616. Highlight down one side of the stems and leaves in stem stitch with DMC 30469.

enlarge illustration by 200%

Copper Cups (*Pileanthus peduncularis*)

Threads Blossoms, 628, 728, 787, 947, 963, 985
DMC Rayon Floss, 30498, 30552, 30742, 33371, 35200

Large flowers Fill in the petals of the flowers with Blossoms 787 and Blossoms 728 in satin stitch. Alternate the colours for the flowers to create shading and texture. Fill the centre of the flower with French knots in DMC 33371, then stitch French knots around the centre in DMC 30552 (Fig. 1). Stitch white French knot highlights in DMC 35200 over the centre and spilling onto the petals (Fig. 2). Highlight around the outside edge of the petals in DMC 30498 in stem stitch (Fig. 3), and then, with DMC 30742, work a lazy daisy stitch between each petal (Fig. 4).

Small flowers Fill in the petals of the flowers with Blossoms 787 and Blossoms 728 in satin stitch. Alternate the colours for the flowers to create shading and texture. Stitch a single French knot in the centre with DMC 30498 and Blossoms 963 threaded in the same needle. Stitch straight stitch highlights on the orange petals in DMC 30742 and in DMC 30498 on the gold-orange petals (Fig. 5). Highlight the outside edge of the petals in DMC 30498, the same way as in the large flowers (Fig. 5).

Buds Fill in some of the buds with satin stitch in Blossoms 787 and the others in Blossoms 728. Work straight stitch highlights on the orange buds in DMC 30742 and in DMC 30498 on the gold-orange buds. Highlight the outside edge of the buds in DMC 30498.

Stems Stem stitch the thin stems in Blossoms 947 and use whipped chain stitch in Blossoms 985 for the thicker part of the stems.

Leaves The leaves are stitched with a 10-wrap bullion and the buds are cupped with a lazy daisy stitch on each side of the bud with Blossoms 628.

fig. 1

fig. 2

fig. 3

fig. 4

fig. 5

enlarge illustration by 200%

fig. 1

fig. 2

fig. 3

Australian Bluebell (*Sollya heterophylla*)

Threads Blossoms, 607; Gemstones, AP3, AP5, AZ1, AZ5, C5
DMC Rayon Floss, 30300, 30322, 30415, 30469, 30841

Flowers Stitch the underneath dark petals with straight stitch in Gemstones AZ5 (Fig. 1), keeping a sharp tip on the petals by going in the same hole. Lay the light petals over the top of the dark ones in the same manner, using Gemstones AZ1. Highlight around one side of the dark petals in DMC 30322 with straight stitch (Fig. 2). Highlight around both sides of the light petals in DMC 30415 with straight stitches.

Buds Stitch the buds with straight stitches in AZ5 and AZ1, laying the colours side by side to create shading. Make some stitches short and others longer (Fig. 3).

Leaves Fill in some of the leaves at the top of the stem with slanted satin stitch in Gemstones C5, then fill in the rest with Blossoms 607. Highlight down the centre of each leaf in stem stitch in DMC 30469. With the same colour, work lazy daisy stitches at the top of each bud.

Stems Stitch the main thick stems in chain stitch with Gemstones AP5, then highlight down one side in stem stitch with DMC 30300. Stitch the fine stems holding the flowers with stem stitch in Gemstones AP3, then highlight down one side in stem stitch with DMC 30841.

enlarge illustration by 200%

Rough Honeymyrtle (*Melaleuca scabra*)

Threads

Blossoms, 059, 636, 637, 983, 985

DMC Rayon Floss, 30839, 30973

Flowers Stitch stamens with uneven straight stitch in Blossoms 059, then stitch French knots at the tip of each stamen with 2 strands of DMC 30973.

Buds Stitch colonial knots with Blossoms 059 and Blossoms 983 threaded in the same needle.

Leaves The leaves are stitched with 10- to 12-wrap bullions in Blossoms 636 and Blossoms 637, alternating the colours to create shading and depth.

Stems Stitch the stems in chain stitch in Blossoms 985, then highlight down one side of the stem with stem stitch in DMC 30839.

Seed pods Stitch a colonial knot for the centre of the pod in Blossoms 985, then stitch 6 very small straight stitches around the colonial knot in Blossoms 983 (Fig. 1).

fig. 1

enlarge illustration by 150%

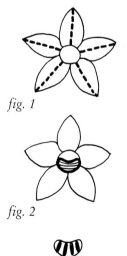

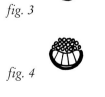

fig. 1

fig. 2

fig. 3

fig. 4

fig. 5

Long-Leaf Wax Flower (Native Daphne) (*Eriostemon myoporoides*)

Threads Blossoms, 637, 990; Gemstones, G5, H4
DMC Rayon Floss, 30367, 30501, 30841, 30976, 33371

Flower Stitch the flowers with a satin stitch slanting into the centre vein of the petal, using Blossoms 990. Highlight down the centre of each petal in back stitch with DMC 30841 (Fig. 1). Stitch the column with padded satin stitch in Blossoms 990 (Fig. 2). Work straight stitch highlights over the column in DMC 30367 (Fig. 3), then stitch French knots at the top of the column in DMC 30976 (Fig. 4). Using the same colour, add straight stitch highlights under the column (Fig. 4).

Buds and half-open flowers Fill the petals of the buds with satin stitch and add the pink highlights in Gemstones H4, as indicated in Fig. 5. Stitch small straight stitches at the bottom of each bud in Blossoms 637.

Leaves Fill the leaves with slanted satin stitch in Blossoms 637, then stem stitch highlights down the centre of the leaves in DMC 30501.

Stems Stitch the stems in slanted satin stitch, getting wider at the bottom of the stems, in Gemstones G5. Highlight down one side of the stems in DMC 33371.

enlarge illustration by 150%

Christmas Bell (*Blandfordia punicea*)

Threads

Blossoms, 646, 648, 708, 827, 869

DMC Rayon Floss, 30498, 33820

Flowers Fill in the bell shape of the flowers with split stitch in Blossoms 827, leaving the lower portion to be stitched with straight stitch in Blossoms 708. Highlight this section in blanket stitch with DMC 33820 (Fig. 1). Stitch the stem of the flower that joins the main stem with Blossoms 827 in stem stitch, then highlight the stem and around the outside edge of the flower with stem stitch in DMC 30498 (Fig. 2). Add straight stitch highlights at the bottom and top of the flower in the same colour.

Thick stems Stitch the thick stems in whipped chain stitch with Blossoms 869.

Leaves Stitch the leaves with very long stem stitches in Blossoms 648 and Blossoms 646, alternating the colours to create shading and depth.

fig. 1

fig. 2

enlarge illustration by 200%

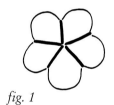

fig. 1

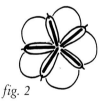

fig. 2

fig. 3

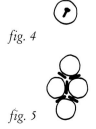

fig. 4

fig. 5

Coastal Bearded Heath (*Leucopogon parviflorus*)

Threads Blossoms, 648, 679, 748, 859, 943, 947, 990
DMC Rayon Floss, 30469, 30841, 30898, 30976

Flowers Fill in the petals with satin stitch in Blossoms 990, with 6–8 stitches to each petal. Stitch a red straight stitch highlight in Blossoms 859 between each petal (Fig. 1). With DMC 30976 stitch a lazy daisy stitch around each red straight stitch coming out from the centre (Fig. 2). Stitch a single French knot for the centre in Blossoms 748.

Buds Fill in the buds with satin stitch in Blossoms 990, working 6–8 stitches for each bud. Add 3 straight stitch highlights at the base of each bud in DMC 30898 (Fig. 3).

Nuts Fill the nuts with padded satin stitch in Blossoms 943, then stem stitch around the outside of the nuts in DMC 30841. Stitch a small pistil stitch in the centre of each nut in DMC 30898 (Fig. 4) and highlight between the nuts in DMC 30898 in back stitch to create shadows (Fig. 5).

Stems Work these in stem stitch at the tips, moving into a slanted satin stitch to make the stems thicker at the base, in Blossoms 947. Highlight one side of the stems in stem stitch with DMC 30898. Stitch the stems at the tip of the nuts in Blossoms 947 in stem stitch and highlight with DMC 30898.

Leaves Fill in the leaves with slanted satin stitch in Blossoms 648 and Blossoms 679, alternating the colours to create shading. Highlight around the outside of the leaves in stem stitch with DMC 30469.

enlarge illustration by 150%

Common Dampiera (*Dampiera linearis*)

Threads

Blossoms, 386, 387, 549, 577, 990
DMC Rayon Floss, 30581, 30798, 30976

Flowers Stitch the petals of the flowers in lazy daisy stitch with Blossoms 386 and Blossoms 387, alternating the colours for the flowers to create shading and depth. Work fly stitch highlights around the outside edge of the petals in DMC 30798 (Fig. 1). Add 3 straight stitch highlights in Blossoms 990 (white) to the lower petals, radiating out from the centre. Stitch a French knot in the centre of the flowers with DMC 30581 and DMC 30976 threaded in the same needle.

Buds Stitch 1–3 lazy daisy stitches for the petals of the buds in Blossoms 386 and Blossoms 387, alternating the colours for the buds to create shading and depth. Stitch fly stitch highlights around the outside edge of the petals in DMC 30798 (Fig. 2). Stitch a straight stitch on either side of the buds in Blossoms 577 and Blossoms 549, alternating the colours to create shading and depth.

Leaves and stems Stitch slanted satin stitch for the leaves (Fig. 3) and stem stitch for the stems in Blossoms 549 and Blossoms 577, alternating the colours to create shading and depth.

fig. 1

fig. 2

fig. 3

enlarge illustration by 200%

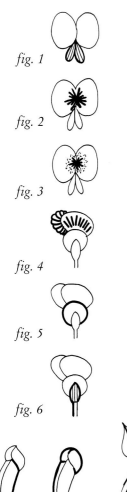

fig. 1

fig. 2

fig. 3

fig. 4

fig. 5

fig. 6

fig. 7 *fig. 8* *fig. 9*

Handsome Flat Pea (*Platylobium formosum*)

Threads Blossoms, 039, 636, 708, 851; Gemstones, AP3
DMC Rayon Floss, 30841, 30895, 33820

Flower Blanket stitch the large petals in Blossoms 708, then fill in the small petals with straight stitches in the same colour (Fig. 1). Work straight stitches radiating out from the centre in Blossoms 039 (Fig. 2). Stitch yellow highlights over the red, using straight stitch in DMC 33820 (Fig. 3).

Buds With blanket stitch, fill in the large petal of the buds in Blossoms 851 and the small petal at the back in Blossoms 039 (Fig. 4). Work some straight stitch highlights on the large petal in Blossoms 039 (Fig. 4). Straight stitch the sepal in Blossoms 636 and stem stitch highlights with DMC 30895 around the top of the sepal (Fig. 5). With Gemstones AP3 straight stitch the calyx, and then, with straight stitches, highlight down each side of the calyx with DMC 30841 (Fig. 6). Fill in the centre of the small green buds with straight stitches in Blossoms 636 and add 3 straight stitches on either side of the bud in Gemstones AP3 for the calyx. Highlight each side with DMC 30841 in straight stitches.

Pea pods Satin stitch the pods in Blossoms 636, then stem stitch highlights down the outside edge in DMC 30895 (Fig. 7). Stitch the calyx with satin stitch in Gemstones AP3. Finish by stem stitching down the outside edge of the pods in Gemstones AP3 (Fig. 8).

Stems Chain stitch the stems in Gemstones AP3 and highlight down one side in stem stitch with DMC 30841.

Leaves Fill in the leaves with slanted satin stitch in Blossoms 636. Highlight the centre vein of the leaf in DMC 30841 in satin stitch, taking the stem stitch part way down the main stem (Fig. 9).

enlarge illustration by 200%

Pink Paper Daisy (*Helipterum roseum*)

Threads

Blossoms, 074, 093, 540, 636, 708, 985

Gemstones, AP5

DMC Rayon Floss, 30501, 30818

Flowers Stitch the outside petals in lazy daisy stitch with Blossoms 074 (Fig. 1), then stitch a second row of petals in Blossoms 093 (Fig. 2), slightly overlapping the outside petals. Highlight the petals with DMC 30818, working a straight stitch radiating out from the centre (Fig. 3). Stitch 1–3 French knots in the middle of the centre with Blossoms 540 (Fig. 4), then stitch a row of French knots on the lower edge of the centre, using Blossoms 708 for the highlight (Fig. 5). Fill in the rest of the centre with French knots in Gemstones AP5 (Fig. 6).

Buds and open buds For the open buds, stitch the outside petals in lazy daisy stitch with Blossoms 093, then stitch a second row of petals in Blossoms 074, slightly overlapping the outside petals. Use straight stitches for the sepal, in Blossoms 636. Fill in the small buds with straight stitch in Blossoms 074 and then add straight stitches on either side and in the centre of the buds with Blossoms 636.

Leaves With Blossoms 636 stem stitch the leaves, then highlight the undersides of the leaves in stem stitch with DMC 30501. Highlight the buds in the same colour in straight stitch, 3 for the small bud and 5 for the open bud.

Stems Stem stitch the stems in Blossoms 985.

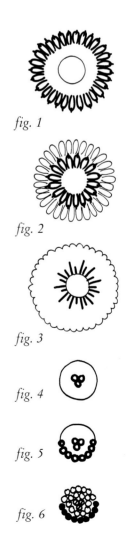

fig. 1

fig. 2

fig. 3

fig. 4

fig. 5

fig. 6

Tea in the Garden

Tea is back in vogue so it is time to stitch a cosy for your teapot. What could be nicer than making a pot of tea with tea leaves, placing your beautiful tea cosy on the pot and inviting a friend around to tea in the garden with scones, jam and cream.

Once again, this design can be used for many other projects, for example, repeated around the edge of a blanket or as single flowers on pyjamas or jumpers, a glasses case, or in the corners of a tea cloth and napkins.

REQUIREMENTS

White wool blanketing, 50cm x 32cm (19 1/2" x 12 1/2")

Backing fabric, 55cm x 35cm (21 3/4" x 13 5/8")

Crewel needle No. 6 (wool thread)

Ribbon in two different colours to match backing fabric,
*   each colour 2m x 3mm (6' 6" x 1/8") cut in 4 x 50cm (19 1/2") lengths*

Bridal white sewing thread to match wool blanketing

Water-soluble pen

Hoop, 15cm (6")

THREADS

Gumnut Blossoms

053	704
055	708
636	823
637	851

Gumnut Jewels

Dark Topaz
Dark Agate

Gumnut Buds

746

DMC Rayon

30676
30754
30957

PREPARATION

Trace the embroidery design and tea cosy outline pattern onto tracing paper. Fold the blanketing in half and mark the fold line with a tacking stitch. Pin and centre the design 5cm (2") from the bottom of the wool blanketing. Make small holes in the tracing paper with an awl or large blunt needle to mark a dot with the water-soluble pen where the flowers are to go. Only mark one flower on at a time, as a lot of dots on the fabric becomes confusing. Keep marking the design as you embroider each section.

STITCHES

Chain stitch
Whipped chain stitch
French knot
Straight stitch
Slip stitch

EMBROIDERY INSTRUCTIONS

All embroidery is worked with a single strand unless otherwise stated. You may like to use a hoop but it is optional. Never leave your embroidery in the hoop when you are not working on it, as the tension may mark the fabric.

Pink flowers With Blossoms 055, stitch the inside petals of the flower in long and short straight stitches. Stitch the outside petals in Blossoms 053, again with long and short straight stitches. Overlap some stitches into the middle petals to blend the two colours together. Fill in the centre with French knots in Jewels Dark Topaz. Highlight the petals in DMC 30957 with long and short straight stitches.

Yellow flowers With Blossoms 708, stitch the inside petals of the flower in long and short straight stitches. Stitch the outside petals in Blossoms 704, again with long and short straight stitches. Overlap some stitches into the middle petals to blend the two colours together. Fill in the centre with French knots in Jewels Dark Agate. Highlight the petals in DMC 30676 with long and short straight stitches.

Apricot flowers With Blossoms 823, stitch the inside petals of the flower in long and short straight stitches. Stitch the outside petals in Blossoms 851, again with long and short straight stitches. Overlap some stitches into the middle petals to blend the two colours together. Fill in the centre with French knots in Buds 746. Highlight the petals in DMC 30754 with long and short straight stitches.

*See enlargement
guide page 174*

Leaves Fill in the leaves with straight stitches. Angle the stitches into the centre vein of the leaf, stitching some leaves in Blossoms 636 and the rest in Blossoms 637, to create shading.

Stems Stitch the stems in whipped chain stitch, some with Blossoms 636 and the rest with Blossoms 637, to create shading.

CONSTRUCTION

Cut out the wool blanketing according to the pattern sheet. Cut the ribbons into 50cm (19 $^1/_2$") lengths (you will have 8 lengths). Place the ribbons in pairs, one of each colour, so that they face inside the cosy, 10cm (4") from the bottom on each side. Stitch the 4 pairs to the sides.

Place the wool and backing fabric right sides together and stitch on the machine, leaving a 10cm (4") opening to turn the tea cosy right side out. Trim the seams, turn right side out and slip stitch the opening closed. You may like to add some cotton wadding to your cosy for extra padding. I make it a habit not to use polyester wadding, because of the likelihood of melting. Set a pretty table outside in the garden and have a nice cup of tea.

enlarge illustration by 150%

Sweet Daisies, Sweet Dreams

A design that will extend your skills in stitching, and advance your skill in shading and creating movement in flowers. The daisies would look attractive stitched on a bag or cushion. These pretty daisies stitched in the middle of a coloured blanket would be a quick and satisfying project. Or you could embroider individual daisies on napkins and placemats or bookmarks, around the neckline of a jumper or on a shopping bag. Any of these ideas would expand the uses for this design. Be adventurous with colour, as this is a versatile design with endless possibilities.

THREADS

*Watercolours
by Caron*

Peacock

DMC Rayon

35200

*Needle Necessities
Perle 5*

5130

*Paterna
Persian Yarn*

260	642
601	732
603	

STITCHES

French knot

Herringbone stitch

Satin stitch

Stem stitch

Whipped stem stitch

Straight stitch

REQUIREMENTS

Pink wool blanketing, 80cm x 30cm (31 1/4" x 11 3/4")

Lining fabric, 90cm x 30cm (35 1/8" x 11 3/4")

White ribbon, 2m x 20mm (6' 6" x 3/4")

Mokuba ribbon 4563, colour No. 9, 1m x 15mm (39" x 5/8")

Crewel needles, No. 6 (wool thread), No. 10 (rayon thread)

Chenille needle, No. 22 (wool thread)

PREPARATION

Fold the blanketing in half lengthwise and mark the fold line with a tacking thread. Place the bottom of the pattern on the right side of the fabric, 1cm (3/8") from the tacking thread. Mark the pattern by piercing holes in the pattern sheet where the flowers are to go with a blue water-soluble fabric marker, or pencil. When you have finished embroidering the flowers, mark in the stems and leaves. When these are completed, mark the bow and complete the embroidery.

EMBROIDERY INSTRUCTIONS

All embroidery is worked with a single strand unless otherwise stated.

Daisies Stitch 3 to 4 straight stitches for the petals on the daisy in Paterna 260. Stitch 3 straight stitch highlights on each petal with DMC 35200, making the middle stitch longer than the others. Stitch French knots in the lower part of the centre in Paterna 732. Fill in the remainder of the centre with French knots in Paterna 642. Highlight the centre by randomly stitching French knots in Needle Necessities 5130.

Buds Stitch the petals on the buds in the same manner as the open flowers, in Paterna 260. Fill in the calyx with satin stitch in Paterna 642, overlapping some stitches into the petals to create a softer effect.

Stems Stem stitch the stems in Paterna 642. Stitch 3 to 4 straight stitches in the same colour at the end of the stems, to join the buds and stems together. Whip the stem stitch on the three stems indicated on the pattern sheet, in Needle Necessities 5130.

Leaves Stem stitch some of the leaves in Paterna 601 and the rest in Paterna 603; this variation will create shading.

Bows Stem stitch around the outline of the bow in Watercolours Peacock, then fill in the bow with herringbone stitch. Fill in the centre knot of the bow with satin stitch in the same colour. Tie a double bow in the Mokuba ribbon and stitch it to the centre of the stitched bow.

CONSTRUCTION OF THE HOT WATER BOTTLE COVER

Cut the lining fabric 90cm x 30cm (35 $^1/_8$" x 11 $^3/_4$"). Fold right sides together lengthwise and machine stitch the side seams. Leave the lining inside out. Place right sides of wool together, sew the side seams and turn right side out. Place the lining on the inside of the hot water bottle cover, push it to the bottom and smooth it out. Tack or pin the lining in position.

There will be 5cm (2") of lining showing above the wool. Turn under a double 2.5cm (1") hem and hand-stitch in place. Stitch the ribbon in place on the side seam where the lining and wool meet. On the side that you tie the bow, blanket stitch a loop to hold the ribbon in place.

Place your hot water bottle in the cover, curl up with a good book and enjoy.

enlarge illustration by 150%

See enlargement
guide page 174

~ 51 ~

Glitz & Dazzle with Crewel

This is the ideal project for the beginner to crewel embroidery, with a smaller variety of stitches than are required for the next item in this book, the 'Spring Awakening Bell Pull'. The colours are bright and fun to stitch on the black fabric. If you haven't had much experience with metallic threads, this is an excellent way to start using them.

If you don't wish to make a footstool, the design would look beautiful as a cushion, or framed, or you could take one small section of the design to stitch on a pincushion or scissors case, for a stunning gift. Use this design to experiment with a variety of textured and coloured fabrics to add new dimensions to your work.

REQUIREMENTS

Wooden footstool
Charcoal black closely woven wool fabric of your choice,
  40cm x 40cm (15 5/8" x 15 5/8")
Calico, 40cm x 40cm (15 5/8" x 15 5/8")
  (only used if padding and covering your own footstool)
Water-soluble Vilene, 40cm x 40cm (15 5/8" x 15 5/8")
Crewel needles, No. 6 (wool thread), No. 8 (metallic thread), No. 10 (beads)
Hoop, 24 cm (9 1/2")
Water-soluble pen
Toy fill

STITCHES

Back stitch	*French knot*
Blanket stitch	*Satin stitch*
Fly stitch	*Straight stitch*

PREPARATION

Transfer the pattern onto the water-soluble Vilene. Tack the Vilene to the fabric in a grid pattern, so that the two pieces of fabric don't move.

EMBROIDERY INSTRUCTIONS

Refer to the design sheet for the number placement of the flowers. Use a single strand of thread unless otherwise stated.

Now place the fabric in the hoop and commence your embroidery.

Mill Hill
Glass seed beads

00020
00557
02012

Mill Hill Antique
glass beads

03034
03053

Mill Hill Frosted
glass beads

62034

Kreinik #4
Metallic Braid

002V	031
150V	041
002HL	042
001	061
005	085
015	093
023	198
024	326
026	684
028	9192

Kreinik #8
Metallic Braid

012	070
027	329
034	829
045	

Paterna
Persian Yarn

311	611
312	630
321	631
322	651
326	692
341	693
342	694
343	703
344	732
521	804
522	815
543	845
600	846
602	904
604	905
610	940

enlarge tracing guide by 120%

stitch guide

Section 1 ~ Pansy

Petals Fill in the middle petals (A) in Paterna 311 in blanket stitch, stitched very close together. Stitch dark shadow highlights in Kreinik #4, 026, using uneven straight stitches. Place more uneven straight stitch highlights over the first layer of stitches in Kreinik #4, 002V.

Fill in the centre petals (B) in Paterna 312 in blanket stitch, stitched very close together. Stitch the highlights in Kreinik #4, 093, using uneven straight stitches. Fill in the centre of the flower with beads 03053 and 00557 mixed together.

Bud Blanket stitch the bud (1A), using Paterna 311 for the areas marked A and Paterna 312 for the area marked B. Highlight A with uneven straight stitch in Kreinik #4, 026, to create a dark shadow. Work more uneven straight stitch highlights over the first layer, using Kreinik #4, 002V. Highlight B in Kreinik #4, 093, with uneven straight stitches.

Leaves and stems Fill in the leaves (C) with satin stitch, using Paterna 600 for the areas marked 1, Paterna 602 for the areas marked 2 and Paterna 604 for the area marked 3. Highlight around the outside edge of the leaf segments in fly stitch, using Kreinik #8, 829. Back stitch the stems in Paterna 604.

Section 2 ~ Cornflower

Petals Fill the large outside petals of both the large and small flowers (A) with satin stitch in Paterna 341. Then fill in the small petals with satin stitch, using Paterna 344 for the petals marked 1, Paterna 343 for those marked 2, and Paterna 342 for the petals marked 3. Add straight stitch highlights around these petals with Kreinik #4, 041. Stitch French knots at the top of the flowers with Paterna 815. Stitch beads 00020 between the French knots.

Leaves and stems Fill in the leaves (B) with satin stitch, using Paterna 692 for those marked 1, Paterna 693 for those marked 2, and Paterna 694 for the leaves marked 3. Back stitch the stems in Paterna 692. Then, using the same colour, stitch small uneven straight stitches for the stamens.

Section 3 ~ Dahlia

Petals Fill in the outside petals (A) with blanket stitch, using Paterna 703. Fill in the pointed petals between the outside petals (B) with long satin stitches, using Paterna 846. Stitch a fly stitch around each pointed petal in Kreinik #4, 9192. Using the same colour, stitch three uneven straight stitches coming up from the base of the petals and going down half-way up the petals. Repeat these steps by stitching over the last steps, using Kreinik #8, 012, to stitch fly stitch around the petals and the three uneven straight stitches coming up from the base of the petal.

Fill in the round inside petals with satin stitch in Paterna 845. Stitch French knots around the top edge of these petals in Kreinik #8, 027.
The centre of the flower is filled with beads 62034 and 00557 mixed together.
Small and medium buds Fill in the buds (D) with satin stitch, using Paterna

845. Fill the centre at the top of the bud with French knots in Paterna 703. Stitch French knot highlights in Kreinik #4, 028.

Leaves and stems Fill in the leaves (E) with satin stitch in Paterna 630 and 631, stitching 2 leaves in 630 and the other 2 in 631. Back stitch the stems in Paterna 631. Highlight down the centre of the leaves with back stitch in Kreinik #4, 015. With the same colour, stitch straight stitches, coming up from the outside of the leaf and going down at the vein. Satin stitch the stamens of the buds (D) in Paterna 631. Highlight the sides of the stamens in Kreinik #4, 015, with straight stitches.

Section 4 ~ Pea

Pea Fill in the part of the pea marked A in satin stitch in Paterna 521.

Peas Fill in the peas (B) in satin stitch in Paterna 940. Fill in the background of the pea shell in satin stitch with Paterna 522.

Sepals Fill in the sepals (C) with satin stitch in Paterna 940. Back stitch down one side of the pods in the same colour. Highlight between the back stitch and pod with another row of back stitch in Kreinik #4, 031. With the same colour, work fly stitches around the sepals and tiny back stitches around the peas.

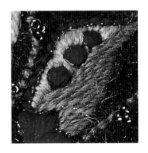

Leaves and stems Fill in the leaves with satin stitch slanted into the vein, using Paterna 522. Highlight the centre vein with back stitches, using Kreinik #4, 198. Back stitch the stems in Paterna 521.

Section 5 ~ Carnation

Flower and buds Fill in the petals (A) with a long satin stitch in Paterna 904. Add cross stitch highlights over the lower part of the petals in Kreinik #4, 326. Repeat these steps for the buds. Fill in the base of the flowers (B) with satin stitch, using Paterna 905. Highlight by stitching uneven straight stitches in Kreinik #4, 024, coming up from the base of the flower and going down two-thirds of the way up. Repeat these steps for the buds. Highlight around the tips of the petals (D) in Kreinik #4, 001, with straight stitches. Place one bead, 03034, at the pointed tip of each petal and bud.

Leaves and stems Fill in the leaves (C) with fly stitches, packed very closely together, in Paterna 651. Using the same colour, fill in the sepals of the buds and flowers with satin stitch. Back stitch the stems in Paterna 651. Highlight around the outside of the leaves in stem stitch, using Kreinik #8, 045.

Section 6 ~ Violet

Petals Fill in the outside petals (A) with blanket stitch in Paterna 321. Highlight the petal with straight stitches in Kreinik #4, 042. Fill in the middle petals (B) with blanket stitch in Paterna 322. Fill in the outside petals of the bud (B) in the same colour with blanket stitch. Fill in the small petals between the large petals (C) with long satin stitches in Paterna 326. Highlight the petals with straight stitches in Kreinik #4, 093. Fill in the middle petal of the bud in

the same manner. Fill the centre of the flower (D) with French knots in Paterna 732. Highlight this with more French knots in Kreinik #4, 002HL.

Leaves and stems Fill 2 leaves (E) in Paterna 610 and the other 2 in Paterna 611, with blanket stitch. Highlight down the centre of the leaves in back stitch with Kreinik #4, 085. Work straight stitch highlights radiating out from the vein in the same colour. Using Paterna 610, back stitch the stems and fill in the sepal (E) of the flower and the bud in satin stitch.

Section 7 ~ Blue and yellow flowers

Flower Blanket stitch the outside petals (A) in Paterna 815. Blanket stitch the middle petals (B) in Paterna 804. Fill in the centre (C) with French knots in Paterna 543. Stitch French knot highlights on top in Kreinik #8, 329. Stitch 3 straight stitches coming out from the top of the flower in Kreinik #8, 329, and add one bead, 00557, to the end of each straight stitch.

Note: The following are attached to the Pansy (Section 1) and the Carnation (Section 5) stems.

7A ~ Medium bud Blanket stitch the outside petals (A) in Paterna 815. Fill in the centre (C) with French knots in Paterna 543. Add French knot highlights on top of those, with Kreinik #8, 329. Stitch 3 straight stitches coming out from the top of the flower and medium bud (D) in Kreinik #8, 329. Add one bead, 00557, to the end of each straight stitch.

7B ~ Small bud Fill in the single petal (A) with blanket stitch in Paterna 815. Fill in the centre at the top of the bud (B) with French knots in Paterna 543. Add French knot highlights on top of those, in Kreinik #8, 329.

7C ~ Tiny buds Satin stitch the petal in Paterna 815. Stitch 3 French knots in Paterna 543 for the centre at the top of the bud. Stitch a single French knot highlight on top of this in Kreinik #8, 329.

7D ~ Sepals Stitch the sepals in straight stitch: in Paterna 600 for the area marked 1, Paterna 602 for the area marked 2, and Paterna 604 for the area marked 3. Highlight around the outside edge of the sepals with a fly stitch, using Kreinik #8, 829. Back stitch the stems in Paterna 604.

Section 8 ~ Butterfly

Fill in the body (A) with small satin stitches in Kreinik #4, 150V. First fill in the main wing (B) in Kreinik #4, 024, with blanket stitch, and then stitch the wing behind it in the same colour in blanket stitch. Fill in the two side wings (C) with blanket stitch in Kreinik #4, 326. Stitch a French knot for the eye in Kreinik #4, 005, and small straight stitches for the feelers in Kreinik #4, 001.

Section 9 ~ Butterfly

Fill in the body (A) with small satin stitches in Kreinik #4, 002HL. To create stripes, stitch straight stitches over the top of this in Kreinik #4, 005. Fill in the front wing (B) with blanket stitch in Kreinik #8, 329, and then fill in the wing behind (C) in blanket stitch in Kreinik #4, 684. Stitch a French knot for the eye in Kreinik #4, 005, and small straight stitches for the feelers in Kreinik #4, 001.

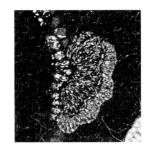

Section 10 ~ Caterpillar

Fill in the body of the caterpillar with small satin stitches in Kreinik #8, 034. Stitch a French knot for the eye in Kreinik #4, 005, and small straight stitches for the feelers in Kreinik #4, 001.

Section 11 ~ Lady bug

Fill in the wings of the bug with satin stitch in Kreinik #4, 061. Fill in the body with satin stitch in Kreinik #4, 005. Stitch the feelers with straight stitches in Kreinik #4, 001.

Clusters of three beads

Using a matching sewing thread, stitch the small clusters of 3 beads, 02012, to the stems.

Note: Now you have finished your embroidery you will have to rinse the fabric very thoroughly to remove all traces of the water-soluble Vilene.

CONSTRUCTION

Remove the plate from the top of the wooden footstool and draw a circle around the plate onto the calico with a water-soluble pen. Cut out the fabric, allowing an extra 4cm to 5cm (1 5/8" to 2") out from the outside edge of the drawn circle. Run a tacking stitch around the outside of the drawn circle with a strong thread (linen or dental floss). Place the wooden plate at the back of the fabric and start to draw the thread tight, leaving enough space to place the toy fill in. Pack the toy fill very tightly. Tighten off the thread and finish with an oversew stitch. Repeat for the embroidered fabric, but without the toy fill. Place the top on the footstool and screw it in place. You may wish to finish the stool top by tacking a braid around the edge. Tuck the ends down the side so that you don't see them, to create a nice neat finish.

Spring Awakening Bell Pull

The beautiful threads in the Sheep's Silk range by The Thread Gatherer add a new dimension to crewel embroidery. The lovely over-dyed shades give the embroidery greater depth, as well as being wonderfully soft to work with.

With the changing nature of the threads' colours, elements of this design could be worked on small projects: pin cushions, scissors keeps, spectacle cases, table linen, evening bags or clothing, or single flowers could be stitched and placed inside a greeting card. You may like to frame your piece, as I have, but it would look lovely stitched as a bell pull.

REQUIREMENTS

Note: If you wish to frame your embroidered piece, add an extra 20cm (8") to the width and length of the fabric.

Linen, 25cm x 75cm (9 3/4" x 29 1/4")

Pellon, 25cm x 75cm (9 3/4" x 29 1/4")

Piping or braid of choice, 1.6m (5' 2 3/8")

Backing fabric of your choice, 25cm x 75cm (9 3/4" x 29 1/4")

Brass bell pull findings for the top and bottom of the bell pull

Crewel needle No. 7 (wool thread)

Hoop, 15cm (6")

Water-soluble pen

Sewing thread to match the fabric

STITCHES

Back stitch	Pistil stitch
Blanket stitch	Satin stitch
Detached blanket stitch	Padded satin stitch
Buttonhole stitch	Slanted satin stitch
Chain stitch	Spider web stitch
Whipped chain stitch	Stem stitch
Coral stitch	Circular stem stitch
Fly stitch	Surface stem stitch
French knot	Whipped stem stitch
German knotted stitch	Straight stitch
Palestrina stitch	Trellis stitch

PREPARATION

Fold your fabric in half lengthways, and finger press. Place the pattern sheet under the fabric, line up the centre of the fabric with the centre of the design sheet and pin the two together. Trace the design onto the fabric with a water-soluble pen or marker of your choice. If you have trouble tracing the design onto the fabric, use a light box or hold the fabric and design up to the light of a window and trace. Tack the Pellon to the back of the fabric, place in a hoop and commence embroidery.

EMBROIDERY INSTRUCTIONS

Refer to the design sheet for the number placement of the flowers. Use a single strand of thread unless otherwise stated.

Now place the fabric in the hoop and commence your embroidery.

The Thread Gatherer: Sheep's Silk

Athens Teal
Berry Spritz
Blue Velvet
Butternut Orange
Chartreuse
Coral
Cotton Candy Dark
Dark Forest
Easter Parade
Fuchsia
Gilded Lavender
Grape Soda
Green Leaves
Greyed Green
Halloween Confetti
Jelly Beans
Kaleidoscope
Lavender Blue
Leaf Green
Leaf Green Dark
Marigold
Mulberry
Old Gold
Patriotic Blue
Pumpkin Orange
Raspberry
Rose
Royalty
Ruby Red
Rusty Amber
Spring Pastela
Stormy Skies
Sun Flowers
Tutti-Frutti
Wisteria

Kreinik Blending Filament

042
045
091

Kreinik #4 Braid

022
026

© 2002 Gail Rogers Kindred Spirits   KS Crewel 1

enlarge tracing guide by 200%

*See enlargement
guide page 174*

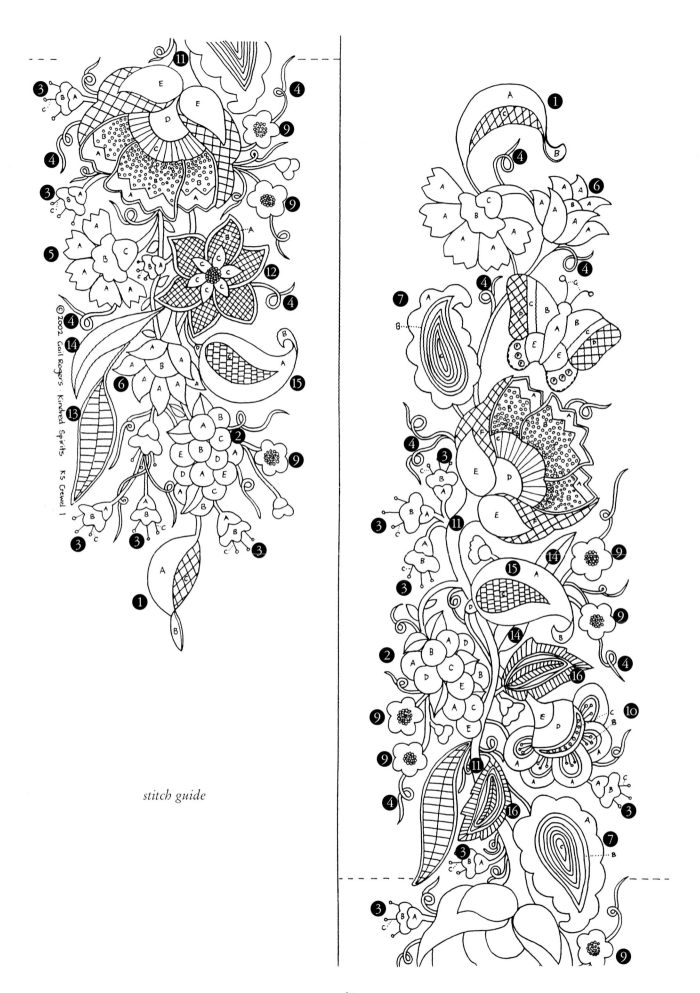

stitch guide

© 2002 Gail Rogers' Kindred Spirits KS Crewel 1

1 Leaf

Fill in the upper portion of the leaf (A) in chain stitch, stitched very closely together, using Chartreuse. Fill in the tip of the leaf (B) in satin stitch in Chartreuse. Back stitch the lower outside edge of the tip in Ruby Red to highlight the tip. The lower portion of the leaf (C) is filled in with trellis stitch in Gilded Lavender and the crosses of the trellis stitch are stitched in Ruby Red. Back stitch the lower outside section of the leaf in Chartreuse, and stitch the stem in chain stitch in the same colour.

Stitch the leaf at the base of the design in the same manner. The trellis stitch is stitched to the right of the leaf and the Ruby Red highlight to the right side of the tip of the leaf.

2 Berries

Stitch the berries in French knots, placed very close together:
(A) Berry Spritz
(B) Fuchsia
(C) Ruby Red
(D) Mulberry
(E) Raspberry

The leaves are stitched in slanted satin stitch, using Dark Forest.

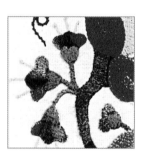

3 Small flower buds

The stem is stitched in whipped chain stitch. The calyx of the flower (A) is filled with satin stitch in Leaf Green. Fill in the petals (B) with blanket stitch, stitched very closely together in Halloween Confetti. Stitch pistil stitches for the stamens at the top of the petals (C) in Marigold.

4 Tendrils

All the tendrils on the design are stitched in coral stitch in Kaleidoscope.

5 Flower

Fill the petals of the flower (A) with satin stitch, stitched very closely together, in Sun Flowers. Fill in the centre of the flower (B) with Royalty in blanket stitch. Stitch the calyx (C) in Chartreuse in stem stitch, stitched very closely together. Stitch the stem in Halloween in stem stitch, adding some extra rows at the base of the flower to create a thicker stem.

6 Flower

Fill in the petals (A) with satin stitch in Wisteria. Stitch the centre (B) in detached blanket stitch in Old Gold. Stitch the stem and calyx in chain stitch in Chartreuse, 2 rows for the stem and extra rows where the stem joins the flower for the calyx.

7 Leaf

Blanket stitch very closely together around the outside edge of the leaf (A) in Jelly Beans. For the section marked B, stitch 1 row of palestrina stitch in Grape Soda, then work 2 rows of chain stitch, 1 in Grape Soda and 1 in Sun Flowers, very closely together on the inside of the leaf. Stitch another row of Palestrina stitch in Grape Soda. Finish the centre of the leaf (C) in satin stitch with Sun Flowers.

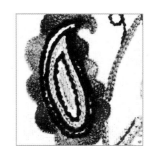

8 Large flower

Stitch the top of the centre petals (A) in blanket stitch in Athens Teal. Fill the bottom of the petals (B) in French knots in Athens Teal, thinning the knots out as you reach the blanket stitch. Fill in the next part of the flower (C) with spider web stitch, in Easter Parade. Fill in the centre of the flower (D) with stem stitch, stitched very closely together, in Marigold. Use circular stem stitch in Raspberry to fill the lower small outside petals (E). Fill the outside petals (F) with satin stitch in Coral, then stitch trellis stitch over the satin stitch in Tutti-Frutti.

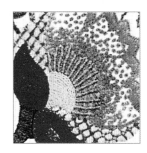

9 Small flowers

Fill in the petals with satin stitch, stitched very closely together, in Lavender Blue. Use French knots in Sunflowers for the centres.

10 Medium flower

Blanket stitch very closely together around the outer edge of the petals (A) in Rose. Stitch chain stitch in Spring Pastela along the inside edge of the blanket stitch. Using Spring Pastela, stitch 3 pistil stitches in the inside of each petal (B). Stitch whipped chain stitch around section C in Sun Flowers, then stitch French knots in the centre in the same colour. Fill in section D in surface stem stitch in Patriotic Blue. Satin stitch section E in Dark Forest.

11 Large stems

Stitch all the large stems in Green Leaves in slanted satin stitch.

12 Small to medium flower

Outline the petals (A) in chain stitch in Patriotic Blue. Fill in the centre of the petals (B) in Rose trellis stitch and the central petals (C) in satin stitch in Easter Parade. Stitch French knots in the centre (D) with Old Gold.

13 Medium leaf

Fill in the centre of the leaf with German knotted stitch, in Stormy Skies. Stitch around the outside of the leaf in stem stitch in Pumpkin Orange. Stem stitch the stem in Stormy Skies.

14 Small to medium leaf

Using Greyed Green, fill in the leaf with fly stitch stitched very closely together so that no fabric shows.

15 Medium leaf

Fill in the outside edge of the leaf (A) with chain stitch in Butternut Orange. Satin stitch the tip of the leaf (B) in the same colour. Stitch the centre of the leaf (C) in buttonhole stitch in Blue Velvet. Stitch the top of the stem (D) in straight stitches, then stitch the rest of the stem in whipped stem stitch in Leaf Green Dark.

16 Medium leaf

Stitch blanket stitch around the outside edge of the leaf in Leaf Green. Next, stem stitch a row in Rusty Amber. Using the same colour, stitch a row of chain stitch. Fill in the centre of the leaf with evenly spaced fly stitch in Leaf Green. Stitch the stem of the leaf in whipped stem stitch in Leaf Green.

17 Butterfly

Fill in the body and head of the butterfly (A) with satin stitch in Kreinik #4, 022. Fill in the wings (B) with satin stitch, using Cotton Candy Dark and Kreinik Blending Filament (BF) 042 threaded in the needle together. With surface stem stitch in Leaf Green, fill in the wing bands (C), then back stitch around the band in Kreinik BF 045. Fill in the outside of the wings (D) with trellis stitch, using Wisteria and Kreinik #4, 026, threaded in the needle together. Kreinik #4, 026, is used to stitch the crosses on the trellis stitch. Fill in the inside edge of the lower part of the wings (E) in satin stitch, with Marigold and Kreinik BF 091 threaded in the needle together, then back stitch around the edge with the same threads. Fill in the dots on the lower wings (F) with padded satin stitch, using Wisteria and Kreinik #4, 026, threaded in the needle together. Back stitch the outline of the lower wing in Marigold. Back stitch the antennae in Kreinik #4, 022. Fill in the ends with tiny satin stitches in the same colour.

CONSTRUCTION

The bell pull should measure 15cm x 65cm (5 7/8" x 25 3/8"). To make it up, first sew the piping or braid down each side of the bell pull. Place the embroidery and backing fabric with their right sides together, and sew down the sides. Turn right side out and press. Pull one end of the bell pull through the findings and hand sew to the back of the bell pull. Repeat for the other end.

Congratulations! Stand back and admire your work.

Bear on a Swing

ust when the bear is having a nice relaxing time on the swing, the Willie Wagtail comes to annoy him, making him go cross-eyed. Can the bear swing high enough to make the Willie Wagtail go away? I think not.

What we have here is one small bear spending a quiet time in the garden, but where are the other four bears? This small bear is the forerunner to the series of bears on blankets and the beginning of the bear stories. He is an excellent beginner project in preparation for the larger designs on blankets to come. This design would also look wonderful on a crib or pram blanket.

RQ5

118

RQ3

enlarge tracing guide by 150%

See enlargement
guide page 174

REQUIREMENTS

White wool blanketing, 80cm x 30cm (31 1/4" x 11 3/4")

Cream wool blanketing, 15cm x 15cm (5 7/8" x 5 7/8")

Lining fabric, 90cm x 30cm (35 1/8" x 11 3/4")

Cream ribbon, 2m x 20mm (6' 6" x 3/4")

Silk ribbon No. 100, 15cm x 4mm (5 7/8" x 3/16")

Crewel needle No. 6 (stranded thread), No. 9 (rayon thread)

Chenille needles, Nos 22, 24 (wool and Watercolours)

Water-soluble pen

Creamy white matching thread

Toy fill

PREPARATION

Fold the white wool blanketing in half lengthways and mark the fold line with a tacking thread. Place the pattern on top of the blanketing 10cm (4") from the tacking. Trace the pattern onto tracing paper. Pierce holes in the pattern sheet with an awl or large blunt needle and then using a fabric marker or pencil mark the positions of the flowers and swing. Only mark one part of the pattern onto the fabric at a time as it is very difficult to follow a multitude of marks on the wool.

EMBROIDERY INSTRUCTIONS

All embroidery is worked with a single strand unless otherwise stated.

Swing and bear

Stitch the swing first in Watercolours Sunset. The posts and seat of the swing are stitched in stem stitch. Then stitch small straight stitches to give texture to the posts and seat. The top of the swing and the chains are worked in chain stitch still using Watercolours Sunset.

Trace the bear from the pattern sheet onto paper or Vilene. Cut the bear shape out pin it to the small piece of coloured blanketing and trace around the outside edge. Cut out and pin the bear onto the blanket sitting on the swing. With a matching thread tack in place very close to the cut edge leaving a small opening. Lightly stuff the bear with a small amount of toy fill through the opening which can then be tacked closed. Blanket stitch the bear in place with 2 strands of DMC 3774 and then using the same colour stem stitch the inside markings for the arms legs and face. Make sure that every third stitch goes through to the back of the wool to give the bear a plump sculptured look. Fill in the nose with satin stitch using DMC 3371 (2 strands) and with small straight stitches stitch the mouth. Stem stitch around the eyes and fill in the pupils with small satin stitches in the same colour (2 strands).

Hydrangea

Fill in the flower heads in Gemstones S2 S3 and S4 with tightly packed French knots. Refer to the pattern sheet for colour placement. Stitch the leaves in Gemstones B5 with fly stitches worked very closely together. The stems are embroidered in Gemstones B5 in stem stitch.

Pink blossoms

Stitch the flower heads in Blossoms 855 with French knots stitched closely together at the base and tapering off towards the top of the blossoms. Stitch French knots at the tip of the blossoms in Gemstones D2 where it is marked with black dots on the design sheet. Place French knots in Blossoms 855 where the black dots are on the design sheet at the base of the flowers.

Stitch the leaves in Gemstones D2 with lazy daisy stitches clustered around the base of the blossoms and stitched closely together. Still with Gemstones D2 stitch a few French knots trailing off at the top of the flowers and at the base of the plant for green grass.

hydrangea

Yellow chrysanthemums

Stitch the flower heads in Blossoms 746 with small straight stitches radiating out from the centre of the flowers. Stitch a French knot in the centre using Marlitt 826. Stitch the stems in Gemstones D2 with stem stitch. Still using D2 stitch small fly stitches down the stems for leaves. Stitch some wood violets in French knots in Blossoms 364 scattered among the bunch of yellow chrysanthemums on the swing seat. Stitch the silk ribbon in place on the bunch of flowers and tie in a bow.

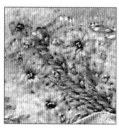

yellow chrysanthemums

Pink climbing rose

Stitch the flowers in Gemstones RQ5 Gemstones RQ3 and Blossoms 118. Follow the pattern sheet for colour placement. Start in the centre of the roses. Stitch 5 small straight stitches going in and out of the same hole and laying the thread first to the left of the centre stitch then to the right of the centre stitch. It takes 5 stitches to complete each petal and there are 5 petals to each flower. The centre is stitched in Gemstones TP5 with a single French knot. The leaves and stems are stitched in Gemstones B5 with stem stitch for the stems and lazy daisy for the leaves coloured black on the design sheet.

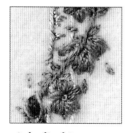

pink climbing rose

Rose buds

The buds are stitched in the same manner and with the same colours as the petals on the roses but only one petal is used to create a bud. See the pattern sheet for colour placement. Stitch around the buds in Gemstones D2 with a fly stitch then stitch another fly stitch a little longer than the first so that you have 2 fly stitches around each bud. Still with Gemstones D2 stitch a lazy daisy at the tip of each bud.

Yellow and white daisies

The daisies are stitched randomly in Blossoms 724 and Blossoms 991 in lazy daisy stitch. The centres are stitched in Marlitt 1077 with a single French knot. Stitch the leaves and stems in Blossoms 645 with straight stitches then scatter French knots throughout the design where the black dots are in the same colour.

Blue wood violets

Stitch the violets in Blossoms 364 in French knots where the dots are at the base of the daisies. The leaves are very small straight stitches worked in Gemstones B5.

Bird

Last but not least stitch the Willie Wagtail on top of the swing in DMC 310 (2 strands). The tail body and head are stitched in satin stitch and the legs are stitched with a small straight stitch.

CONSTRUCTION OF THE HOT WATER BOTTLE COVER

Cut the lining fabric 90cm x 30cm (35 $^1/_8$" x 11 $^3/_4$"). Fold right sides together lengthwise and stitch the side seams. Leave the lining inside out. Place right sides of the wool blanketing together sew the side seams and turn right side out. Place the lining on the inside of the hot water bottle cover push it to the bottom and smooth it out. Tack or pin the lining in position. There will be 5cm (2") of lining showing above the wool. Turn under a 2.5cm (1") hem and hand-stitch in place. Stitch the ribbon in place on the side seam where the lining and wool meet. On the side that you tie the bow blanket stitch a loop to hold the ribbon in place.

Well done! Your hot water bottle is complete so snuggle up and enjoy it.

May Bears

baby blanket

Bear No. 1 is trying to take off on the maypole without much luck. He can't seem to get off the ground and can't understand that maybe it's because he eats too much honey. Bear No. 2 is lying in the grass watching a bee, quite oblivious to what is happening around him, wondering if bees sting. I think this is a very dreamy bear, don't you?

Bear No. 3 is the only one up, up and away on the ribbons of the maypole and very pleased with himself indeed. Do you think he will stay up there very long?

Bear No. 4 is sulking and sitting with his back to everyone as he doesn't want to play this game and is missing out on so much fun — and there is not even any honey to make him happy. Bear No. 5 is looking confused as to how he managed to fall off and land in the garden bed on his bottom with such a thud. Then we have the little blue bird flying around with the extra ribbon from the maypole and having a lovely time joining in the game. Can you find the spider?

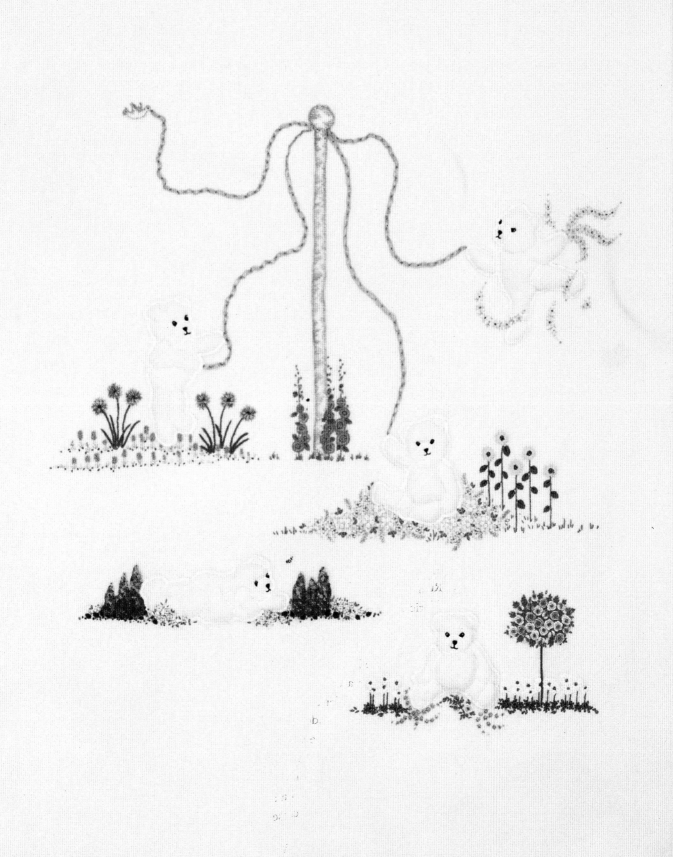

THREADS

Appletons Crewel Wool

141	741
292	742
293	743
342	751
343	752
352	753
353	754
461	877
471	891
551	892
547	893
552	894
642	911
643	951
692	

Anchor Marlitt

800	895
801	898
826	1059
827	1077
868	1207
879	1212

Paterna Wool

260	703
262	

Kreinik Blending Filament

032

DMC Stranded Cotton

310	3371
842	

Watercolours by Caron

Gobi Sands

REQUIREMENTS

Cream wool blanketing, 1.1m x 80cm (43" x 31 1/4")

Extra wool blanketing for the bears, 50cm x 20cm (19 1/2" x 8")

Printed fabric, 1.3m x 1m (50 3/4" x 39")

Ivory piping, 3.8m (12' 6")

Chenille needles, Nos 22, 24 (wool thread)

Crewel needles, No. 8 (wool thread), 9 (rayon thread and Kreinik)

Straw needle No. 6 (bullions)

Water-soluble pen

Hoops, 15cm (6") and 23cm (9")

Small amount of toy fill to stuff the bears

YLI silk ribbon, 141 (pale brown), 3m x 4mm (9 3/4' x 1/8")

STITCHES

Blanket stitch	*Lazy daisy*
Bullion	*Lazy daisy bullion*
Colonial knot	*Satin stitch*
Couching stitch	*Slanted satin stitch*
Fly stitch	*Stem stitch*
French knot	*Straight stitch*

INSTRUCTIONS FOR CUTTING OUT, PLACEMENT AND ORDER OF WORKING

It is advisable to mark and work one section of the flowers or design at a time, as it is very difficult to follow a multitude of marks on the fabric.
Run a large tacking thread down the middle and across the centre of the wool fabric to mark the centre of the blanket. Trace the maypole and hollyhock design onto tissue paper. Pin the design of the maypole to the centre of the blanket (the bottom of the maypole should be 40cm [15 5/8"] from the bottom of the blanket). Make holes in the pattern sheet and through them mark dots with a water-soluble pen, to show the position of the maypole on the fabric. Embroider the maypole. Next, mark the placement of the hollyhocks and embroider them. Trace the bears from the pattern sheet onto paper or Vilene. Cut the shapes out and pin them to the small piece of blanketing. Trace around the bears and cut them out. Pin the bears in place, then tack very closely around the edge of each bear, leaving a small opening. Lightly stuff each bear with a small amount of toy fill through the opening, which can then be tacked closed.

Bear No. 2

See enlargement
guide page 174

Bear No. 1

Bear No. 4

Bear No. 3

Bear No. 5

EMBROIDERY INSTRUCTIONS FOR MAYPOLE

Use a single strand of thread unless otherwise stated.

The maypole is stitched in Watercolours Gobi Sands (1 strand) in blanket stitch. Stitch the blanket stitch unevenly, making the stitches long, medium and short. This will create a shaded effect down the sides of the maypole (refer to the design).

Threads Appletons, 642, 741, 754; Anchor Marlitt, 868, 879, 1059 DMC, 310, 842; Kreinik, 032; Watercolours, Gobi Sands

Hollyhocks Stitch the hollyhocks in blanket stitch using Appletons 754, leaving a small circle in the middle of the flower for the centre French knots. Stitch a quarter-circle in blanket stitch for the buds at the top of the hollyhocks, in Appletons 754. Stitch French knots in Appletons 754 where the black dots are on the design sheet. The rest of the French knots are stitched in Appletons 642 to create shading.

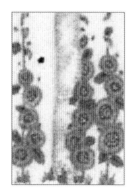

maypole & hollyhocks

With Marlitt 879 (2 strands), stitch 5 French knots in the centre of each flower. Using Appletons 642, fill in the leaves with slanted satin stitch, facing into the vein of the leaf (Fig. 1), stem stitch the stems and stitch the grass in long and short straight stitches.

Spider and web Create the spider web by stitching straight stitches in Kreinik 032. Anchor the intersections of the web down with small straight stitches.

Using DMC 310 (1 strand) stitch the spider's body with French knots, then stitch the legs with very tiny straight stitches.

fig. 1

Bird Using Appletons 741 and Marlitt 1059 (1 strand of each) threaded in the needle together, stitch around the outside of the bird in stem stitch, and with a long and short satin stitch, fill in the wings and the tail. The eye is stitched with a single colonial knot in DMC 310 (2 strands). The beak is stitched with 2 tiny straight stitches to form a small V shape in Marlitt 868.

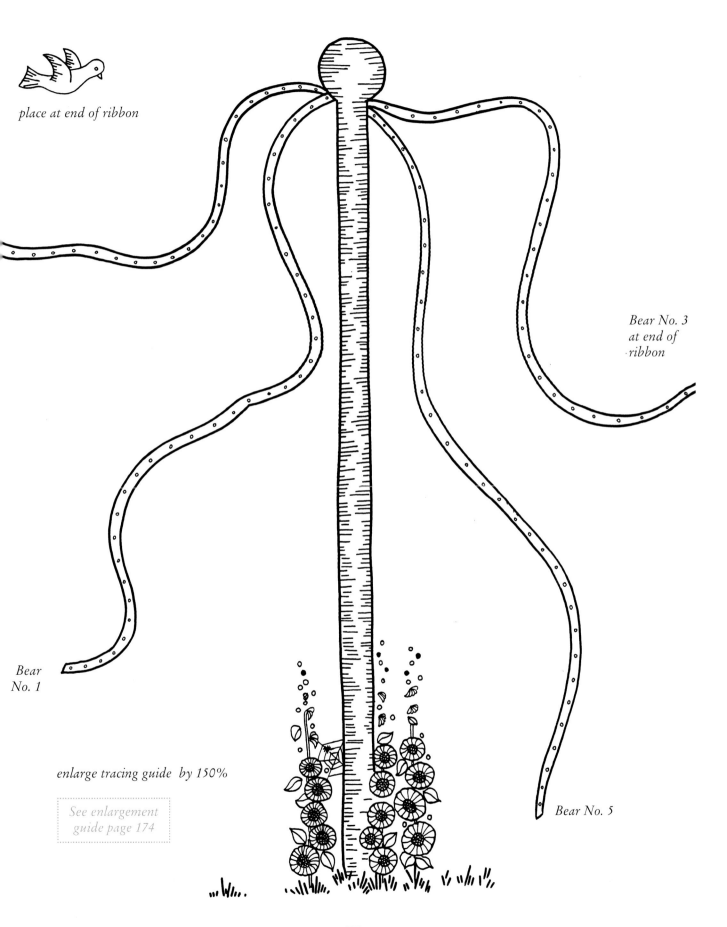

place at end of ribbon

Bear No. 3
at end of
ribbon

Bear
No. 1

enlarge tracing guide by 150%

See enlargement
guide page 174

Bear No. 5

fig. 2

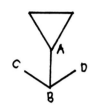

fig. 3

bear mouth & nose

EMBROIDERY AND APPLIQUÉ INSTRUCTIONS FOR BEARS

Use a single strand of thread unless otherwise stated.

Blanket stitch the bears to the blanket with 2 strands of Marlitt 1212, making sure that the stitches are small and even. Stem stitch the lines for the legs, arms and head with 2 strands of Marlitt 1212, taking every third stitch through to the back of the blanket and using a stabbing motion to give the bear shape.

Using DMC 3371 (2 strands), stitch around the eyes with a very small stem stitch and fill in the pupils with small satin stitches.

Fill in the nose with satin stitch in DMC 3371 (2 strands), then add a straight stitch across the top of the nose to give it a nice shape, coming up at A and going down at B (Fig. 2).

Using DMC 3371 (2 strands), stitch a straight stitch coming out at A, going down at B, coming up at C, going down at B, coming up at D and going down at B (Fig. 3).

Illustrations for bears should be enlarged. An enlargement guide for photocopying is on page 174.

PLACEMENT GUIDE FOR APPLIQUÉING BEARS

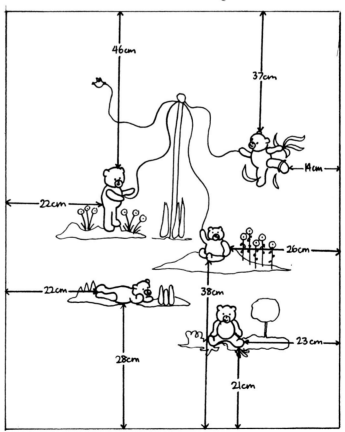

CONSTRUCTION OF THE FINISHED BLANKET
Refer to page 174 for instructions.

enlarge illustration by 200%

Bear No. 1

Threads
Appletons, 141, 293, 352, 461, 743
Anchor Marlitt, 895, 1212
DMC, 3371

Agapanthus With Appletons 461 and 743 threaded together in the same needle, stitch long and short fly stitches for the petals (Fig. 4). Then add straight stitches between each petal, radiating out from the centre, in Appletons 293 (Fig. 5).

For the leaves, stitch two rows of stem stitch, placed very close together, in Appletons 293. Start the second row one stitch lower than the first row to create a tip at the top of the leaf. Scatter French knots around the bottom of the plant in Appletons 293. Stitch the stems with whipped stem stitch in the same colour.

Pink hyacinths Fill in the hyacinths with French knots, using Appletons 141. Stitch the stems in Appletons 352 with small straight stitches, then stitch French knots in Appletons 293 around the flowers. With Appletons 352 stitch the lower leaves in small straight stitches. With Marlitt 895, stitch small straight stitches for the upper leaves. Scatter French knots around the flowers in the same colour.

fig. 4

fig. 5

agapanthus

enlarge illustration by 200%

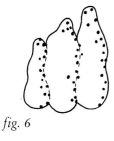

fig. 6

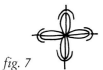

fig. 7

larkspurs

Bear No. 2

Threads Appletons, 342, 551, 547, 552, 891, 892, 893, 894
Anchor Marlitt, 801, 868, 898, 1212; DMC, 3371; Kreinik, 032

Larkspurs The larkspurs are stitched with French knots using Appletons 894, 893, 892 and 891. Stitch the darker shade at the bottom, then medium dark, medium light and light at the top. Make this somewhat haphazard to create a more realistic look for the flowers. Stitch the leaves with Appletons 547 in a tiny slanted satin stitch (see Fig. 1 above). With the same colour, scatter French knots throughout the flowers to create shading. The French knots are marked with black dots on the design sheet and in Fig. 6.

Buttercups Use Appletons 552 to embroider some of the flowers and Appletons 551 for the rest, to create shading. Stitch 3 small straight stitches, going in and out of the same hole, for each petal. Stitch 4 petals for each flower. Using Marlitt 868, stitch a fly stitch around each petal (Fig. 7), and a single French knot for the centres of the flowers. Scatter French knots throughout the design in Appletons 552 and 551.

The leaves are stitched in small lazy daisy stitches in Appletons 342, and French knots in this colour are also scattered throughout the design.

enlarge illustration by 200%

Bee The body of the bee is stitched in bullion stitches, placed close together, in Marlitt 801 and 898 (Fig. 8):

3-wrap bullion in Marlitt 801
4-wrap bullion in Marlitt 898
5-wrap bullion in Marlitt 801
5-wrap bullion in Marlitt 898
5-wrap bullion in Marlitt 801
4-wrap bullion in Marlitt 898
3-wrap bullion in Marlitt 801

Stitch a single colonial knot for the head and a small straight stitch for the sting in black. With Kreinik 032, stitch 2 lazy daisy stitches, 1 inside the other, for each wing.

fig. 8

Bear No. 3

Threads
Appletons, 353, 471
Anchor Marlitt, 827, 1077, 1212
DMC, 3371

Yellow daisies Stitch the petals of the daisies in Appletons 471 in lazy daisy stitch. With Marlitt 827 and 1077 (1 strand of each threaded in the same needle), stitch a single French knot in the centre of each daisy.

Stitch the leaves in Appletons 353 with very small straight stitches, then with the same colour scatter French knots between the daisies.

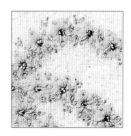

daisies

enlarge illustration by 150%

Bear No. 4

Threads Appletons, 292, 293, 643, 741, 742, 751, 753, 754, 877, 911
Paterna, 260; Anchor Marlitt, 800, 827, 868, 1077, 1212; DMC, 3371

Roses The roses and buds of the topiary are stitched with bullion stitches.
Place the rose and bud combinations, described below, randomly throughout
the rose topiary design and the spray between the legs of the bear:

roses

Rose 1
Centre of the rose — 2 x 5-wrap bullions in Appletons 754
Middle petals — 4 x 7-wrap bullions in Appletons 751
Outside petals — 6 x 9-wrap bullions in Appletons 877

Rose 2
Centre of the rose — 2 x 5-wrap bullions in Appletons 754
Middle petals — 4 x 7-wrap bullions in Appletons 753
Outside petals — 6 x 9-wrap bullions in Appletons 751

Buds Stitch the middle 2 bullions of the bud close together. Place the next 2
bullions slightly lower, meeting at the bottom of the first 2. Finally, stitch the
last 2 bullions lower again, meeting at the base of the bud. This will give
shape to the bud and make the centre stand up and out.

Bud 1
Centre of the bud — 2 x 5-wrap bullions in Appletons 754
Middle petals — 2 x 7-wrap bullions in Appletons 751
Outside petals — 2 x 9-wrap bullions in Appletons 877

Bud 2
Centre of the bud — 2 x 5-wrap bullions in Appletons 754
Middle petals — 2 x 7-wrap bullions in Appletons 753
Outside petals — 2 x 9-wrap bullions in Appletons 751

Stitch a fly stitch around the buds in Appletons 293 for the calyx.

Stems and leaves of roses Embroider the leaves in lazy daisy stitch. Work
some in Appletons 293 and the rest in Appletons 292, to create shading. With
Appletons 911, stitch 2 rows of stem stitch side by side for the stem. Stem
stitch the stem of the rose lying between the feet of the bear in Appletons 293.

Shasta daisies Using Paterna 260, stitch 8 to 9 lazy daisy stitches as the
petals for each daisy. With Marlitt 800, stitch a fly stitch around the outside
edge of each petal (see Fig. 7 above). Mix 2 strands of Marlitt 868 with 1
strand of Marlitt 827 (three strands together in the same needle), and stitch 3
to 4 French knots in the centre of each flower.

daisies

With Appletons 643, stem stitch the stems on the Shasta daisies. Fill in
around the daisies with leaves stitched in lazy daisy stitch in Appletons 643.

Forget-me-nots Stitch the forget-me-nots with 5 French knots stitched in a
close circle in Appletons 742 and Appletons 741. Use the darker colour for the
centre flowers and the lighter colour for those on the outside. Stitch the centre
of the forget-me-nots in Marlitt 1077 (2 strands) with a single French knot.

enlarge illustration by 200%

Bear No. 5

Threads

Appletons, 293, 342, 552, 692, 742, 751, 752, 951

Paterna, 260, 262, 703

Anchor Marlitt, 826, 827, 868, 1077, 1212

DMC, 3371

fig. 9

Daisies With Paterna 262, stitch 5 petals for each daisy in lazy daisy stitch. Add a straight stitch in the middle of each petal in Paterna 260 (Fig. 9). Work a fly stitch around the outside of each of the petals in Appletons 742 (see Fig. 7 above). For the centre of each daisy, stitch a single French knot in Paterna 703.

Small pink flowers Stitch 3 small straight stitches, going in and out of the same holes, for each of the 4 petals. Use Appletons 752 for some flowers and Appletons 751 for the rest. This will give you mixed shading in your flowers. You may like to mix both colours in some of the flowers to create more shading. Work a fly stitch (see Fig. 7 above) around each of the petals in Marlitt 1207. Thread Marlitt 1207 and 826 (1 strand of each) in the needle together and stitch a single French knot in the centre of each flower.

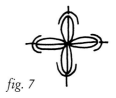

fig. 7

Leaves and fern Scatter lazy daisy stitches in Appletons 342 throughout the design. Stitch a lazy daisy stitch in Marlitt 826 around the outside of each leaf. For the fern, use Appletons 951 to stitch small fly stitches on a slight curve, with a straight stitch at the tip of the fern.

Scattered knots Scatter French knots in Appletons 692 and Marlitt 1077, threaded together in the same needle, throughout the design.

garden

Sunflowers The sunflowers are stitched in 5-wrap lazy daisy bullion stitch, using Appletons 552, with 10 to 11 petals to each sunflower. Thread Marlitt 827 (2 strands) and Marlitt 868 (1 strand) in the same needle together and stitch 6 to 8 French knots in the centres of the sunflowers.

Stitch the leaves in slanted satin stitch (see Fig. 1 above) in Appletons 293. Work the stitches on a slant into the vein of the leaf. Using the same colour, stem stitch the stem and work long and short straight stitches for the grass.

sunflowers

Ribbons Place the ribbons on after you have completed all the embroidery. Lay the silk ribbon 141 onto the blanket and pin in place. Take the ribbon through to the back of the blanket and stitch it in place with matching sewing thread. Couch the ribbon to the front of the blanket with French knots in DMC 842 (2 strands).

Honey 'B' Bears

Bear No. 1 is running very fast and has no idea why the bees are chasing him. He thinks that if he runs through the flowers the bees will get distracted and busy themselves making honey from the flowers. Bear No. 2 can't understand why the bees are making such a fuss. He remembers that someone told him that bees don't like water, so he decides to sit in the pond in the hope that the bees will go away and chase someone else. I wonder if they will.

Bear No. 3 … well, what do you think? I think he is the bear that has stirred up all the bees to try and steal their honey. As they come out of their hive they don't see him, and they go off to chase the other bears. Bear No. 4 is at it again, lying in the garden enjoying all the flowers, with no idea that the other bears are in trouble with the bees — happy little bear. Bear No. 5 is very happy too today as he has a whole pot of honey to himself. If he stays hidden in the flowers he won't have to share it! Do you think he should share? Can you find the spider?

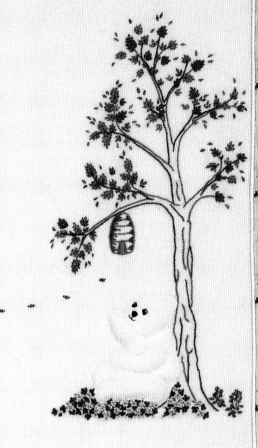

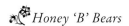

THREADS

Paterna
Persian Yarn

260	691
311	692
341	701
342	703
403	713
433	723
434	725
442	733
504	751
522	754
544	770
545	815
601	830
602	841
603	842
604	905
611	912
612	914
613	915
651	934
652	935
653	944
661	945
662	946
663	950

DMC Rayon Floss

30310	30738
30367	30798
30368	30814
30469	30839
30472	30973
30501	30976
30543	33687
30603	33820
30676	35200

Paterna Wool

260	703
262	

Kreinik
Metallic Thread
032 pearl

DMC
Stranded Cotton
3371

Anchor Marlitt
Rayon Thread
1212 x 2 skeins

REQUIREMENTS

White wool blanketing, 1.1m x 80cm (43" x 31 1/4")

White wool blanketing for the bears, 50cm x 20cm (19 1/2" x 8")

Printed fabric for backing, 1.3m x 1m (50 3/4" x 39")

Cream piping, 3.8m (12' 6")

Small amount of toy fill to stuff the bears

Straw needle No. 7 (bullions)

Crewel needle, No. 6 (stranded thread), No. 9 (rayon thread)

Chenille needle, Nos. 22, 24 (wool thread)

Water-erasable pen

Hoops of different sizes (it is not essential to use a hoop)

Sewing machine thread to match the piping

STITCHES

Blanket stitch

Bullion stitch

Couching stitch

Fly stitch

French knot

Holding stitch

Lazy daisy stitch

Bullion lazy daisy

Pistil stitch

Satin stitch

Padded satin stitch

Slanted satin stitch

Stem stitch

Whipped stem stitch

Straight stitch

PLACEMENT GUIDE
FOR APPLIQUÉING BEARS

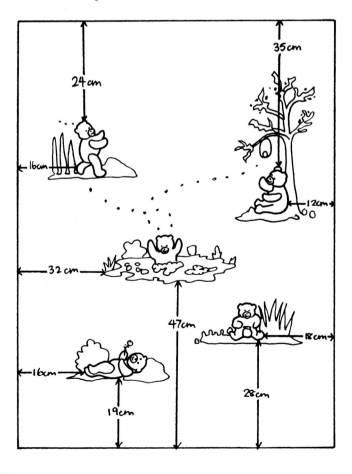

enlarge tracing guides by 150%

Bear No.2

Bear No. 1

See enlargement
guide page 174

Bear No. 4

Bear No. 3

Bear No. 5

INSTRUCTIONS FOR CUTTING OUT AND PLACING BEARS

Run a large tacking thread down the middle and across the centre of the wool fabric to mark the centre of the blanket. Trace the bears from the pattern sheets onto paper or Templastic and cut them out. Pin the bear shapes to the small piece of blanketing, trace around the outside and cut them out. Place the bears onto the blanket using the photo and placement illustration as a guide, remembering that the backing fabric folds over 5cm (2"). Pin the bears in place, then tack very closely around the edge of each bear, leaving a small opening. Lightly stuff each bear with a small amount of toy fill through the opening, which can then be tacked closed.

fig. 1

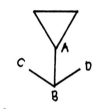

fig. 2

EMBROIDERY AND APPLIQUÉ INSTRUCTIONS

It is advisable to mark and work one section of the flowers or design at a time, as it is very difficult to follow a multitude of marks on the wool. Use a single strand of thread at all times unless otherwise stated.

Blanket stitch the bears to the blanket with 2 strands of Marlitt 1212, making sure that the stitches are small and even. Stem stitch the lines for the legs, arms and head with 2 strands of Marlitt 1212, taking every third stitch through to the back of the blanket, using a stabbing motion, to give the bear shape.

Using DMC Stranded 3371 (2 strands), stitch around the eyes with a very small stem stitch, then fill in the pupils with small satin stitches.

With DMC Stranded 3371 (2 strands), fill in the nose with satin stitch and then add straight stitch across the top of the nose to give it a nice shape, coming up at A and going down at B (Fig. 1).

For the mouth, stitch a straight stitch coming out at A, going down at B, coming up at C, going down at B, coming up at D and going down at B in DMC Stranded 3371 (2 strands) (Fig. 2).

llustrations for bears should be enlarged. An enlargement guide for photocopying is on page 174.

bear mouth & nose

CONSTRUCTION OF THE FINISHED BLANKET
Refer to page 174 for instructions.

enlarge illustration by 200%

Bear No. 1

Threads Paterna, 341, 342, 601, 602, 651, 652, 703, 754, 770
DMC Rayon, 30738, 30798, 30973; DMC Stranded, 3371
Anchor Marlitt, 1212

Daffodils Stitch 4 to 5 petals in lazy daisy stitch with Paterna 703, then stitch a straight stitch in the centre of each petal (Fig. 1). For the centre, stitch a single 10-wrap bullion in Paterna 770. Pick up a small amount of fabric so that the bullion forms a loop. Catch the bullion down with a small holding stitch in the same colour (Fig. 2). Highlight each petal in DMC 30973 by stitching a fly stitch around the petals (Fig. 2). Stitch some of the stems and leaves in Paterna 651 and the rest in Paterna 652, to create shading. Stitch the stems in stem stitch and the leaves in a long lazy daisy stitch with a long tail (Fig. 3).

Delphiniums Stitch the flower petals in lazy daisy stitches in Paterna 342 on the lower flowers, and then stitch the flowers at the top of the design in Paterna 341. Stitch French knots at the top of the design in the same colour. Place a pistil stitch between each petal in DMC 30798 (Fig. 4). Finish with a single French knot in the centre of each flower in Paterna 754 and DMC 30738 threaded together in the same needle. Stem stitch the stems in Paterna 601 and the lower leaves in the same colour with a lazy daisy stitch. Change the colour to Paterna 602 to stitch the upper leaves. With Paterna 602 stitch French knots where there are black dots on the design sheet. Stitch the grass in Paterna 602 in straight stitches.

Bees See instructions for bees in Bear No. 3 below. These can be worked once other embroidery has been completed.

fig. 1

fig. 2

fig. 3

fig. 4

91

fig. 1

fig. 2

fig. 3

fig. 4

fig. 5

Bear No. 2

Threads Paterna, 260, 311, 504, 601, 602, 603, 604, 611, 612, 613, 733, 815, 944, 945; DMC Rayon, 30367, 30368, 30469, 30738, 33687, 35200; DMC Stranded, 3371; Anchor Marlitt, 1212

Water Stem stitch around the water outline in Paterna 504 and stem stitch the ripples in the same colour.

Waterlilies With Paterna 945 stitch 8 petals with 3 straight stitches to each petal, going in and out of the same hole, and laying the thread to the left and the right of the centre stitch (Fig. 1). Using Paterna 944, stitch a straight stitch between each petal (Fig. 2). Finish with a single French knot for the centre of the flower, using Paterna 733 and DMC 33687 threaded together in the same needle. Stitch the leaves in blanket stitch with Paterna 611 and 612, changing the colour for different leaves to create shading. Highlight the leaves in DMC 30367 by stitching long and short straight stitches radiating out from the centre of the leaves (Fig. 3).

Arum lily Stitch the petals in satin stitch in Paterna 260. Stitch a 6- to 7-wrap bullion, coming up at the base of the petal and going down half-way along the petal, in Paterna 815 (Fig. 4). With DMC 35200, stem stitch highlights around each flower. Fill in the leaves with a slanted satin stitch (Fig. 5), alternating Paterna 602 for one leaf and Paterna 601 for the next leaf. Stitch the stems in the matching colours with stem stitch. Stitch the stems of the flowers in the same manner, then finish with a fly stitch at

enlarge illustration by 200%

the base of each flower (Fig. 6). Highlight the centre vein of the leaf in DMC 30469 with a small stem stitch (Fig. 7).

Reeds Stem stitch the reeds and highlight down one side of the reed in stem stitch. To create shading, use Paterna 604 highlighted with DMC 30368 for some reeds and Paterna 603 highlighted with DMC 30367 for the rest.

Irises Stitch the petals with 4 lazy daisy stitches in Paterna 311. With Paterna 260, stitch a straight stitch radiating out from the centre of the flower and going half-way down the petals (Fig. 8). Stitch a single French knot in the centre of each flower with DMC 30738. Straight stitch the leaves and stems in Paterna 612 and 613, alternating the colours to create shading. Finish with straight stitch highlights stitched over the leaves and stems in DMC 30469. You may like to couch these stitches down.

Bees See instructions for bees in Bear No. 3 below. These can be worked once other embroidery has been completed.

fig. 6

fig. 7

fig. 8

Bear No. 3

Threads
Paterna, 403, 433, 434, 602, 603, 604,
611, 703, 723, 912
DMC Rayon, 30310, 30472, 30676, 33820
Kreinik Metallic Thread, 032 pearl
DMC Stranded, 3371
Anchor Marlitt, 1212

Tree and leaves Stitch the trunk in Paterna 433 and
Paterna 434 in stem stitch, changing the colours with the
different lines on the trunk and branches to create shading.
With 3 shades of Paterna — 602, 603 and 604 — stitch
the leaves in lazy daisy stitch, alternating the colours to
create shading. Stitch the tail of the lazy daisy stitch
slightly longer and coming off to one side, to create
movement in the leaves.

Bee hive With Paterna 723 stem stitch around the
outlines of the bee hive, then fill in the door of the hive
with satin stitch in the same colour. Create shading with
Paterna 403 by stitching short straight stitches at the sides
of the bee hive.

Bees The body of each bee is worked in bullion stitch,
stitched closely together, in DMC 33820 and DMC 30310:
3 wrap bullion in DMC 33820
4 wrap bullion in DMC 30310
5 wrap bullion in DMC 33820
5 wrap bullion in DMC 30310
5 wrap bullion in DMC 33820
4 wrap bullion in DMC 30310
3 wrap bullion in DMC 33820

Black — Yellow

3 4 5 5 5 4 3 wraps

fig. 1

fig. 2

Stitch a single colonial knot in black for the head and a small straight
stitch for the sting. The wings are stitched with Kreinik 032 with 2 lazy
daisy stitches, 1 inside the other, for each wing (Fig. 1).

Waldsteinia termata (small yellow flowers) Stitch 5 French knots in a
circle in Paterna 703. Using DMC 30472, stitch pistil stitches between
each French knot petal (Fig. 2). With Paterna 703 and DMC 30472
threaded together in the same needle, stitch a single French knot in the
centre of each flower. With the same threads, stitch the buds scattered
throughout the design in French knots. Stitch the leaves in Paterna 611
with lazy daisy stitches, then stitch small straight stitches for the stems on
the buds in the same colour.

Primulas With Paterna 912, stitch 5 tiny straight stitch petals for each
flower. Stitch a single French knot for the centre of the flowers in DMC
30676. Stitch the leaves in lazy daisy stitches in Paterna 603 and straight
stitch the stems.

enlarge illustration by 200%

enlarge illustration by 150%

Bear No. 4

Threads

Paterna, 260, 442, 602, 603, 653, 661, 662, 691, 692,
701, 713, 725, 841, 842
DMC Rayon, 30543, 30814, 30976, 33820, 35200
DMC Stranded, 3371
Anchor Marlitt, 1212

fig. 1

Sunflowers Stitch the petals of the sunflowers in Paterna 713 with a 4-wrap bullion lazy daisy stitch. Highlight the centre of each lazy daisy petal with a straight stitch in DMC 33820 (Fig. 1). Fill in the centre of the flowers with 6 to 7 French knots in DMC 30976 and Paterna 442 threaded together in the same needle. With Paterna 662 and 661, stitch the stems in a whipped stem stitch and the leaves in slanted satin stitch (Fig. 2). Alternate the colours to form shading for the leaves and stems.

fig. 2

Nasturtiums Fill in the petals in blanket stitch, using Paterna 841 and 842 and alternating the colours to form shading. Stitch 3 small straight stitches on the 3 upper petals in Paterna 701 for the highlights (Fig. 3). Thread DMC 30543 and 30976 in the same needle and stitch a single French knot in the centre of each flower. Fill in the leaves with blanket stitch with Paterna 691 and 692, alternating the colours to form shading. Highlight the leaves with small straight stitches radiating out from the centre of each leaf in DMC 30543 (Fig. 4), finishing with a single French knot in the centre in the same colour.

fig. 3

fig. 4

Rock roses With Paterna 260, stitch 5 petals in padded satin stitch. Start at the base of the petal in the centre of the flower (Fig. 5), come up at A and go down at B. For the next stitch come up at A, lay the thread to the right of the first stitch and go down at B. Next, come up at A, lay the thread to the left of the first stitch and go down at B (Fig. 6). Lay 2 more stitches across the petal. Stitch a fly stitch around the tips of the petals in DMC 35200, then stitch small straight stitches radiating out from the centre in DMC 30814. Finish with a single French knot in Paterna 725 (Fig. 7). For the leaves, stitch lazy daisy stitches, some in Paterna 602 and some in Paterna 603 to create shading, then stitch the trailing buds in French knots in Paterna 653.

fig. 5

fig. 6

fig. 7

sunflowers

nasturtiums

rock roses

enlarge illustration by 150%

Threads

Paterna, 403, 522, 544, 545, 601, 602, 612, 613, 663, 723, 751, 830, 905, 912, 914, 934, 935, 946, 950

DMC Rayon, 30501, 30603, 30839

DMC Stranded, 3371

Anchor Marlitt, 1212

Foxgloves Stitch the foxgloves in lazy daisy stitches hanging down. Fill in the centre with a straight stitch, then finish with a French knot at the tip. Stitch a French knot highlight on the existing French knot at the end of each petal in DMC 30603 (Figs 1, 2 & 3). The colours are as follows:

Flower A Petal — Paterna 914; centre straight stitch — Paterna 912; French knot highlight — DMC 30603

Flower B Petal — Paterna 935; centre straight stitch — Paterna 934; French knot highlight — DMC 30603

Flower C Petal — Paterna 946; centre straight stitch — Paterna 905; French knot highlight — DMC 30603

Stitch the stems and leaves in Paterna 522 and 663, alternating the colours to create shading. For the leaves stitch 3 straight stitches for each leaf, making the middle stitch longer than the 2 outside stitches (Fig. 4). Stitch the stems in stem stitch, and then, alternating the same colours, stitch small straight stitches between the petals of the flowers. Finish with French knots at the tips in the same colour (Fig. 5). Highlight the leaves with 2 straight stitches in DMC 30501 (Fig. 6) worked over the top of the existing stitches.

Grape hyacinths Fill in the bulk of the flower heads with French knots in Paterna 545. Finish with some French knots in Paterna 544 toward the top of each flower (Fig. 7). Stitch the stems and leaves in Paterna 613 and 612 with straight stitches, alternating the colours to create shading.

Helenium autumnale (red flowers) Stitch 5 lazy daisy petals hanging down, alternating Paterna 950 and 830 for the flowers (Fig. 8). Thread DMC 30839 (2 strands) and Paterna 751 in the needle together (making 3 strands) and stitch a French knot at the top of the petals for the centre of the flowers. With Paterna 601 and 602, stitch straight stitches for the stems and long lazy daisy stitches with long tails for the leaves (Fig. 9).

Honey pot Stitch around the outside of the honey pot, and fill in the base of the pot, with stem stitch in Paterna 723. With the same colour, stitch small open blanket stitches to create the shading at the bottom of the pot. Stitch the writing and the shading at the top of the pot in Paterna 403, with small straight stitches.

fig. 1

fig. 2

fig. 3

fig. 4

fig. 5

fig. 6

fig. 7

fig. 8

fig. 9

Coming Ready-or-not

In this blanket the same five bears are playing hide and seek. Bear No. 1 is hiding behind the quilts on the line and thinks no-one can see him. What do you think? I think his feet are showing, so I wonder if Bear No. 4 will see him first. Bear No. 2 is hiding a little bit better but maybe Bear No. 4 can see his tummy between the poles of the seat. I hope he doesn't squash the little flowers in his excitement not to be found.

Bear No. 3 is hiding very well and I think he is going to be last to be seen, as hiding behind the pot is a very good idea. Bear No. 4 is cheating a little, don't you think, as he is peeking from behind his hands. Maybe he was peeking the whole time and now just pretended to cover his eyes. What is happening over the head of Bear No. 4? Is he just too busy peeking at his friends to notice? Do you think mother will be happy when she sees a big flat patch in her beautiful garden? Bear No. 5 thinks he is hiding very cleverly in the garden, but he is too busy smelling the flowers and watching his friend, the bee. Do you think he will be the first bear to be seen by Bear No. 4? Is there a little spider in this design too?

THREADS

Gumnut Blossoms

019	629
033	634
035	635
039	645
053	646
054	678
055	679
055	704
057	706
073	708
157	726
257	748
297	766
299	787
557	809
567	827
586	829
587	869
589	947
606	949
607	966
608	990
626	999
627	

Gumnut Gemstones

AP5	E5
AZ5	S2
B4	S3
C1	S4
C5	S5
D5	

DMC Rayon Floss

30498	30898
30580	33687
30726	33820
30742	35200
30841	

Anchor Marlitt Rayon Thread
827
1037 x 2 skeins
1078

Watercolours by Caron
Flagstone
Kelp
Maple
Tobacco

REQUIREMENTS

Champagne wool blanketing, 1.1m x 80cm (43" x 31 1/4")

Tan wool blanketing for the bears, 50cm x 20cm (19 1/2" x 8")

Printed fabric for backing, 1.3m x 1m (50 3/4" x 39")

Cream piping, 3.8m (12' 6")

Small amount of toy fill to stuff the bears

Straw needle No. 7 (for bullions)

Crewel needle, No. 6 (wool thread), No. 9 (rayon thread)

Chenille needles Nos 22 and 24 (wool thread and Watercolours)

Tapestry needle No. 24 (cross stitch)

Water-erasable pen

Fabric of choice for the cross stitch quilts, 30cm x 15cm (11 3/4" x 5 7/8")

(I used 28 count stitched over two threads — 14 count)

Fabric to back the cross stitch quilts, 30cm x 15cm (11 3/4" x 5 7/8")

Sewing machine thread to match the wool blanketing

Dusty pink thread to match embroidered roses

Hoops of different sizes (it is not essential to use a hoop)

THREADS

Kreinik Blending Filament
032 pearl

DMC Stranded Cotton
310
3371

Dinky Dye Threads
04 Strawberry Ice
10 Cloudy Sky
12 Lemon Sherbet
35 Madi's Rose
42 Opal
25 Ruby
22 Sapphire
32 Sunflower

STITCHES

Back stitch
Blanket stitch
Bullion stitch
Colonial stitch
Cross stitch
Fly stitch
French knot
Granitos stitch
Holding stitch
Lazy daisy stitch
Lazy daisy bullion stitch
Satin stitch
Slanted stitch
Spider stitch
Split stitch
Stem stitch
Straight stitch

enlarge tracing guides by 150%

See enlargement
guide page 174

Bear No. 3

Bear No.2

Bear No. 1

PLACEMENT GUIDE FOR APPLIQUÉING BEARS

Bear No. 4

Bear No. 5

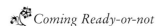

INSTRUCTIONS FOR CUTTING OUT AND PLACING BEARS

Run a large tacking thread down the middle and across the centre of the wool fabric, to mark the centre of the blanket. Trace the bears from the pattern sheet onto paper or Templastic and cut out the shapes. Pin the paper or Templastic to the small piece of blanketing, trace around the shapes and cut them out. Place the bears onto the blanket using the photo and the placement illustration as a guide, remembering that a 5cm (2") border will be covered by the backing fabric turnover. Pin the bears in place, then tack very closely around the edge of each bear, leaving a small opening. Lightly stuff each bear with a small amount of toy fill through the opening, which can then be tacked closed.

fig. 1

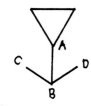

fig. 2

EMBROIDERY AND APPLIQUÉ INSTRUCTIONS FOR BEARS

It is advisable to mark and work one section of the flowers or design at a time, as it is very difficult to follow a multitude of marks on the wool. Use a single strand of thread at all times unless otherwise stated.

Blanket stitch the bears to the blanket, using 2 strands of Marlitt 1037 and making sure that the stitches are small and even. Stem stitch the lines for the legs, arms and head with 2 strands of Marlitt 1037, taking every third stitch through to the back of the blanket, using a stabbing motion, to give the bear shape.

With DMC Stranded 3371 (2 strands), stitch around the eyes with a very small stem stitch, then fill in the pupils with small satin stitches.

Fill in the nose with satin stitch in DMC Stranded 3371 (2 strands), then add a straight stitch across the top of the nose to give it a nice shape, coming up at A and going down at B (Fig. 1).

Again using DMC Stranded 3371 (2 strands), stitch a straight stitch, coming out at A, going down at B, coming up at C, going down at B, coming up at D and going down at B (Fig. 2).

llustrations for bears should be enlarged. An enlargement guide for photocopying is on page 174.

bear mouth & nose

CONSTRUCTION OF THE FINISHED BLANKET
Refer to page 174 for instructions.

Bear No. 1

Threads Gumnut Blossoms, 299, 567, 608, 646, 809, 827, 829
DMC Rayon, 30498, 30742, 35200; DMC Stranded, 3371
Anchor Marlitt, 827, 1037, 1078; Watercolours, Kelp

Clothesline With Watercolours Kelp, stitch the right-hand side of the
clothesline posts in uneven blanket stitch, then stitch down the left-hand
side of the posts in stem stitch. Stitch the line in stem stitch using the
same colour.

Creeper on the left-hand post (*Convolvulus tricolour*) Fill in the flowers
with blanket stitch in Blossoms 299. Highlight the centre with straight
stitches in DMC Rayon 35200. Stitch a single French knot in the centre in
DMC Rayon 30742. The buds are stitched with 3 blanket stitches in
Blossoms 299. Stitch a small fly stitch with a short tail around the buds in
Blossoms 567 (Fig. 1). Stem stitch the stem and stitch lazy daisy stitches
for the leaves in Blossoms 567.

Creeper on the right-hand post (Trumpet Vine/Creeper) Using 3
colours of Blossoms — 809, 827 and 829 — stitch the flowers in an
uneven blanket stitch. Use the colours randomly throughout the design,
to create shading. Highlight with straight stitches angled into the centre
of the flower, in DMC Rayon 30498. Stitch a single French knot in the

fig. 1

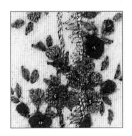

enlarge illustration by 200%

centre with Marlitt 827 and 1078 threaded in the needle together. The buds are stitched with 3 blanket stitches, in Blossoms 809, 827 and 829. Use the colours randomly throughout the design, to create shading. Stitch a small fly stitch with a short tail around the buds in Blossoms 608. Stem stitch the stem in Blossoms 608 and, in the same colour, stitch lazy daisy for the leaves.

Grass Stitch the grass with uneven straight stitches in Blossoms 646.

Quilts on clothesline For the quilts I used Jobelan even weave fabric, but you may like to use a small scrap of even weave fabric that you have on hand. Refer to the cross stitch patterns for the design and count for the small quilts. Place together the right sides of each little quilt and its backing fabric. Machine or hand stitch around them, leaving a small opening. Turn right side out through the opening, which can then be closed, using slip stitch. The quilts are not attached to the blanket until all other embroidery is finished. Stitch them to the top of the line, then stitch the pegs in place. The pegs are made with small straight stitches in Watercolours Kelp. A small holding stitch is stitched across the centre of the peg in the same colour (Fig. 2). Catch the quilts in place by pulling them together where the bear is holding his hands together. Stitch to create some creases on the quilts, to make them look more natural. Hide your anchoring stitches between the cross stitches, so that the stitches don't show.

fig. 2

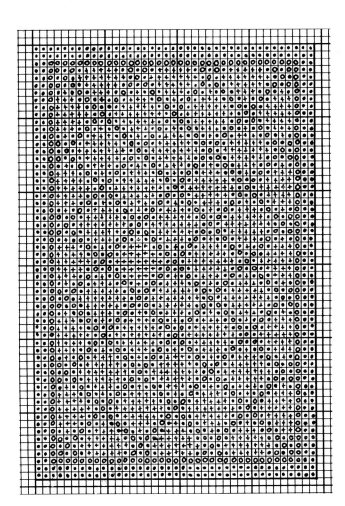

Irish Chain

39 stitches across, 59 stitches down.
Stitched on 28 count.

- •   32 Sunflower
- **o**   22 Sapphire
- **+**   12 Lemon Sherbet

Sunshine & Shadows

43 stitches across, 69 stitches down.
Stitched on 28 count.

- ✕   25 Ruby
- **l**   35 Madi's Rose
- **ø**   04 Strawberry Ice
- **·**   12 Lemon Sherbet
- **o**   22 Sapphire
- **╱**   10 Cloudy Sky
- **—**   42 Opal

Bear No. 1
CROSS STITCH INSTRUCTIONS

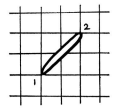
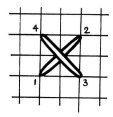

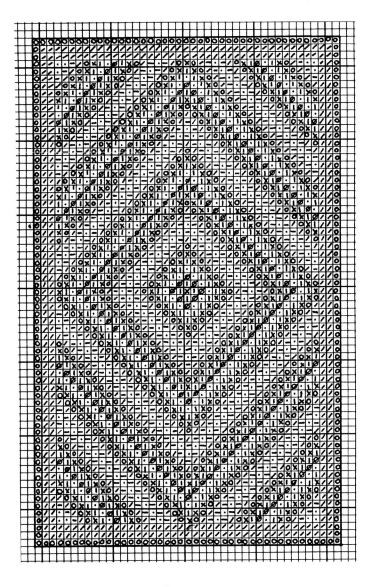

enlarge illustration by 200%

Bear No. 2

Threads Gumnut Blossoms, 019, 297, 567, 586, 587, 589, 646, 679, 708, 869; DMC Rayon, 30580, 30841; DMC Stranded, 310, 3371; Anchor Marlitt, 1037; Watercolours, Flagstone; Kreinik, 032

Rustic log bench Stitch the bench in Watercolours Flagstone in uneven blanket stitch, with stem stitch for the poles. Stitch around the lower and side edges of the seat in a tiny blanket stitch in the same colour. Stem stitch around the top edge of the seat, then stitch some straight stitch shadows in Watercolours Flagstone (Fig.1).

Hyacinths Embroider some hyacinths from the 'Flower 1' instructions and the rest as 'Flower 2', placing them randomly to create shading.
Flower 1 Embroider with French knots in Blossoms 297. For the leaves and stems, stitch 2 straight stitches, stitched very close together, in Blossoms 589. Finish with French knots scattered on the flower heads, in Blossoms 589.
Flower 2 Embroider with French knots in Blossoms 019. For the leaves and stems, stitch 2 straight stitches, stitched very close together, in blossoms 586. Finish with French knots scattered on the flower heads, in Blossoms 586.

Sunflowers Each sunflower has 12 to 16 petals. Stitch lazy daisy bullions of 4 to 5 wraps for each petal in Blossoms 708, leaving a circle in the centre of each flower. Fill in the centres with French knots, using one strand each of Blossoms 869, DMC Rayon 30580 and 30841, threaded in the needle together (3 threads altogether).

Buds Each sunflower bud has 4, 5 or 6 petals. Stitch lazy daisy bullions of 4 to 5 wraps for each petal in Blossoms 708, leaving a slight curve at the base of each bud. Stitch straight stitches for the sepals in Blossoms 567.

Seed Pods Fill in the heads of the seed pods with French knots, using one strand each of Blossoms 869, DMC Rayon 30580 and 30841, threaded in the needle together. Stitch small straight stitches in Blossoms 567 for the sepals of the seed pods.

Stems and leaves Stitch the stems in stem stitch in Blossoms 679, making the stems thicker at the base of the flower (Fig. 2). Fill in the leaves with slanted satin stitches in Blossoms 587, facing the stitches into the centre vein of the leaf (Fig 3.)

Grass Stitch the grass with uneven straight stitches in Blossoms 646.

Spider and web Create the spider web by stitching straight stitches in Kreinik 032. Anchor the intersections of the web with small straight stitches (Fig. 4). Using DMC Stranded 310, stitch the spider's body with French knots. Add the legs, using very tiny straight stitches.

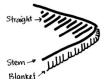

Straight →
Stem →
Blanket →

fig. 1

fig. 2

fig. 3

fig. 4

Bear No. 3

Threads Gumnut Blossoms, 033, 035, 039, 608, 629, 646, 966, 999
Gumnut Gemstones, AZ5, C1
DMC Rayon, 30898, 33687
DMC Stranded, 3371
Anchor Marlitt, 1037
Watercolours, Maple, Tobacco

Urn Stem stitch the outlines of the urn in Watercolours Maple (Fig. 1). Add straight stitches for the shading in the same colour, then fill in the rim at the top and bottom of the urn with satin stitch, using Watercolours Maple (Fig. 2). Fill in the rest of the urn with split stitch in Gemstones C1.

Brick paving Stitch the horizontal lines of the paving in stem stitch with Watercolours Tobacco. With the same colour, stitch 3 straight stitches, getting shorter with each stitch, for the vertical shadows.

Violets Stitch the flowers with single French knots in Gemstones AZ5. Using Blossoms 629 and Blossoms 646, stitch single French knots around the flowers to create shading.

fig. 1

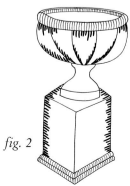

fig. 2

Poppies Stitch Granitos stitch for the flower heads in Blossoms 039, then stitch a single French knot in Blossoms 999 for the centre of the flower. Stitch the buds with Granitos stitch using Blossoms 039 and 608. Some of the buds are red and some are green unopened buds. Stitch 2 small straight stitches around the base of the red buds in Blossoms 608. Stitch the stems in back stitch and the leaves in small straight stitches in Blossoms 608.

Grass Stitch the grass with uneven straight stitches in Blossoms 646.

Rose Stitch the spokes of the rose in a sewing thread that matches the rose colour. Fill in the rose with spider stitch in Blossoms 033. Stitch a single French knot in the centre of each rose with Blossoms 035. Highlight the lower edge of the rose in DMC Rayon 33687, to create shadows. For the buds, stitch 3 tiny straight stitches, stitched closely together, in Blossoms 035. Stitch a fly stitch around each bud, alternately using Blossoms 629 and Blossoms 646, to create shading. The leaves are stitched with lazy daisy stitch in Blossoms 629 and 646, alternating the colours to create shading. Stem stitch the stems in Blossoms 629 and 646, alternating the colours to create shading. In the same colour, stitch 2 rows

enlarge illustration by 200%

enlarge illustration by 200%

of stem stitch at the base of each stem, to create thickness. With DMC 30898, stitch small straight stitches up the side of the stems and on sections of the leaves that join the stems. This will highlight the leaves and stems and give the rose more depth.

Dirt in urn The dirt in the urn is made with French knots in Blossoms 966. Stitch some violets, as instructed above, on the dirt and overlapping the edge of the urn, to create interest.

enlarge illustration by 200%

Bear No. 4

Threads
Gumnut Blossoms, 057, 073, 257, 299, 557, 646, 708, 766, 787, 990
Gumnut Gemstones, D5, E5, S2, S3, S4, S5
DMC Rayon, 30310, 33820, 35200
DMC Stranded, 3371
Anchor Marlitt, 1037
Watercolours, Tobacco
Kreinik, 032

Brick flowerbed Stitch the horizontal lines of the bricks in stem stitch in Watercolours Tobacco. With the same colour, stitch 3 straight stitches, getting shorter with each stitch, for the vertical shadows.

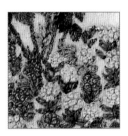

Hydrangeas Fill in the flower heads with tightly packed French knots in Gemstones S2, S3, S4 and S5. Refer to the design sheet for colour placement. Stitch the leaves in Gemstones D5 in satin stitch, angling the stitches into the centre vein of the leaf. The stems are stitched in Gemstones D5 with stem stitch.

Marigolds Fill in the flower heads of the marigolds with French knots in Blossoms 708, 787 and 766, alternating the colours throughout the design. Using Gemstones E5, stitch the stems in straight stitch and the leaves in lazy daisy.

Petunias Blanket stitch the flower heads in Blossoms 057, 073, 257, 299 and 990, following the placement shown on the design sheet. With a single strand each of DMC Rayon 35200 and 33820 threaded in the needle together, stitch a single French knot for the centre. Stitch the leaves with lazy daisy stitch in Blossoms 557.

Bees The body of the bee is stitched in bullion stitches, stitched closely together, in DMC 33820 and 30310 (Fig. 1):

3 wrap bullion in DMC 33820
4 wrap bullion in DMC 30310
5 wrap bullion in DMC 33820
5 wrap bullion in DMC 30310
5 wrap bullion in DMC 33820
4 wrap bullion in DMC 30310
3 wrap bullion in DMC 33820

Black   Yellow

3 4 5 5 5 4 3 wraps

Stitch a single colonial knot for the head and a small straight stitch for the sting in black. The wings are 2 lazy daisy stitches, 1 inside the other, for each wing, in Kreinik 032.

Grass Stitch the grass with uneven straight stitches in Blossoms 646.

enlarge illustration by 200%

Bear No. 5

Threads Gumnut Blossoms, 053, 054, 055, 057, 157, 606, 607, 626, 627, 629, 634, 634, 635, 645, 646, 678, 704, 706, 708, 748, 827, 947, 949, 990; Gumnut Gemstones, AP5, C5
DMC Rayon, 30310, 33687, 33820; DMC Stranded, 3371
Anchor Marlitt, 726, 1037, 1078; Kreinik, 032

Hollyhocks Each flower is worked in the same way, using colour variations to create movement. Flower A gives full details of the stitches used.

Flower A

1   Stitch the lower flower heads in an uneven blanket stitch in Blossoms 704.
2   Stitch the flower heads at the top in uneven blanket stitch in Blossoms 706 (darker on design sheet).
3   For the small buds at the top of the plant, stitch 3 small uneven blanket stitch stitches for each bud in Blossoms 706 (Fig. 1).
4   Stitch French knots at the top of the plant (lighter on design sheet) in Blossoms 706.
5   Stitch uneven straight stitch highlights radiating out from the centre of the flowers in Marlitt 1078.
6   Stitch a single French knot in the centre of the flowers with one strand each of Blossoms 827 and Marlitt 726, threaded in the needle together.
7   Stitch the leaves in an uneven blanket stitch in Blossoms 626.
8   Stitch the stem in stem stitch in Blossoms 626.
9   Stitch a French knot for the green buds scattered throughout the design in Blossoms 626 (darker on design sheet).
10 Stitch 2 lazy daisy stitches and a French knot at the top of each small coloured bud, in Blossoms 626, where the lazy daisy stitches meet (Fig. 1).

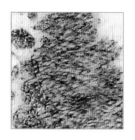

Flower B

1   Lower flower heads: uneven blanket stitch in Blossoms 706.
2   Top flower heads: uneven blanket stitch in Blossoms 708 (darker on the design sheet).
3   Small buds at top of plant: uneven blanket stitch in Blossoms 708 (Fig. 1).
4   French knot buds at top of plant: Blossoms 708 (lighter on design sheet).
5   Highlights: straight stitch in Marlitt 1078.
6   Centre: French knot in Blossoms 827 and Marlitt 726.
7   Leaves: uneven blanket stitch in Blossoms 627.
8   Green buds: French knots in Blossoms 627 (darker on design sheet).
9   Stem: stem stitch in Blossoms 627.
10 Stitch 2 lazy daisy stitches and a French knot at the top of each small coloured bud, in Blossoms 627, where the lazy daisy stitches meet (Fig. 1).

fig. 1

Flower C

1 Lower flower heads: uneven blanket stitch in Blossoms 055.
2 Top flower heads: uneven blanket stitch in Blossoms 057 (darker on the design sheet).
3 Small buds at top of plant: uneven blanket stitch in Blossoms 057 (Fig. 1).
4 French knot buds at top of plant: Blossoms 057 (lighter on design sheet).
5 Highlights: straight stitch in DMC Rayon 33687.
6 Centre: French knot in Blossoms 827 and Marlitt 726.
7 Leaves: uneven blanket stitch in Blossoms 627.
8 Green buds: French knots in Blossoms 627 (darker on design sheet).
9 Stem: stem stitch in Blossoms 627.
10 Stitch 2 lazy daisy stitches and a French knot at the top of each small coloured bud, in Blossoms 627, where the lazy daisy stitches meet (Fig. 1).

Flower D

1 Lower flower heads: uneven blanket stitch in Blossoms 053.
2 Top flower heads: uneven blanket stitch in Blossoms 054 (darker on the design sheet).
3 Small buds at top of plant: uneven blanket stitch in Blossoms 054 (Fig. 1).
4 French knot buds at top of plant: Blossoms 054 (lighter on design sheet).
5 Highlights: straight stitch in DMC Rayon 33687.
6 Centre: French knot in Blossoms 827 and Marlitt 726.
7 Leaves: uneven blanket stitch in Blossoms 626.
8 Green buds: French knots in Blossoms 626 (darker on design sheet).
9 Stem: stem stitch in Blossoms 626.
10 Stitch 2 lazy daisy stitches and a French knot at the top of each small coloured bud, in Blossoms 626, where the lazy daisy stitches meet (Fig. 1).

Flower E (same as Flower C)

Flower F

1 Lower flower heads: uneven blanket stitch in Blossoms 054.
2 Top flower heads: uneven blanket stitch in Blossoms 055 (darker on the design sheet).
3 Small buds at top of plant: uneven blanket stitch in Blossoms 055 (Fig. 1).
4 French knot buds at top of plant: Blossoms 055 (lighter on design sheet).
5 Highlights: straight stitch in DMC Rayon 33687.
6 Centre: French knot in Blossoms 827 and Marlitt 726.
7 Leaves: uneven blanket stitch in Blossoms 626.
8 Green buds: French knots in Blossoms 626 (darker on design sheet).
9 Stem: stem stitch in Blossoms 626.
10 Stitch 2 lazy daisy stitches and a French knot at the top of each small coloured bud, in Blossoms 626, where the lazy daisy stitches meet (Fig. 1).

fig. 1

Trees

Tree A

Fill in the tree shape with split stitch, using Blossoms 634 for the darker section on the design sheet. Fill in the rest of the tree with Blossoms 635, in split stitch. Fill in the trunk with stem stitch in Blossoms 947.

Tree B

Fill in the tree with lazy daisy stitches in Blossoms 645 and Blossoms 646. Stitch clusters of 3 lazy daisy stitches, packed closely together, in each colour. Place the clusters randomly until the tree is filled in. The trunk of this tree is behind the bear.

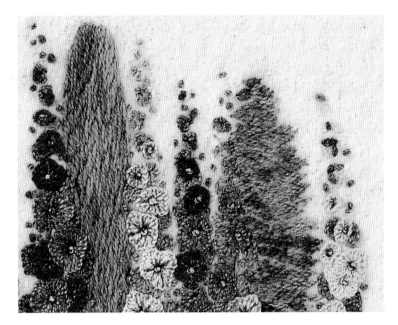

Tree C

Fill in the tree with split stitch in Blossoms 678; for the darker section on the design sheet use Gemstones C5, blending the two colours together to create shading. Satin stitch the trunk in Blossoms 949.

Tree D

Fill in the tree with short straight stitches stitched on a horizontal angle, blending Blossoms 607 and 606 together to create shading. Fill in the trunk with slanted satin stitch in Gemstones AP5.

fig. 2

Rock roses For the 5 petals of each flower, stitch 5 straight stitches, going in and out of the same hole, in Blossoms 990. Lay the threads to the left and to the right of the middle stitch (Fig. 2). Stitch a tiny straight stitch to each petal in Blossoms 157, then finish with a single French knot in Blossoms 748 for the centre. Stitch the large buds with 5 straight stitches to each petal, going in and out of the same hole (Fig. 2), in Blossoms 990. Stitch the rows of small buds in French knots, in Blossoms C5. Using Blossoms 629, stitch fly stitches with tails around the large and small buds (Fig. 3). Stitch lazy daisy leaves in the same colour.

fig. 3

Grass Stitch the grass with uneven straight stitches in Blossoms 646.

Bee Stitch the same as the bees in Bear No. 4 on page 113 (Fig. 4).

Black   Yellow

3 4 5 5 4 3 wraps

fig. 4

Gingerbread Men Blanket

This is a wonderful beginner's project and is very quick to stitch. The felt used in this design makes the gingerbread men look like yummy little biscuits just ready to be picked off the blanket. The gingerbread men have different expressions on their faces and two of the biscuits have sad faces, as they have been picked to be eaten first. You may like all your gingerbread men to have happy faces. With the extra felt you could make a little stuffed gingerbread man to go with the blanket.

REQUIREMENTS

Cream wool blanketing, 1.1m x 80cm (43" x 31 1/4")

Printed backing fabric, 1.3m x 1m (50 3/4" x 39")

Thick tan-coloured plush felt, 1.1m x 15cm (43" x 5 7/8")

Chenille needles, Nos 18 (wool thread), 24 (Watercolours)

Crewel needle No. 6 (stranded thread)

Water-soluble pen

Hoop 15cm (6") (for trellis stitch)

STITCHES

Blanket stitch   *Lazy daisy stitch*

Chain stitch   *Straight stitch*

Colonial knot   *Trellis stitch*

French knot

PLACEMENT INSTRUCTIONS

Make a template from cardboard or Templastic of the smiling gingerbread man and cut it out. Place the gingerbread man template onto the tan felt and trace around the outside of the template with a water-soluble pen. Cut out 8 gingerbread men from the tan felt, making sure that all the gingerbread men face the same way. Run a large tacking thread down the middle and across the centre of the wool blanket to mark the centre of the blanket. Pin the gingerbread men on the blanket in the shape of an oval, as shown in the photo and the diagram. Tack the gingerbread men in place, very close to the edge, with a single strand of DMC Stranded 436, the same colour as the felt. Trace the basket pattern onto a piece of card or Templastic and cut it out. Place the basket design on the blanket between the gingerbread men. Mark around the edge with a water-soluble pen. Repeat 8 times. Mark dots where the French knots will be placed between the baskets. Commence embroidery.

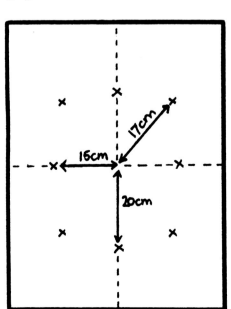

THREADS & BUTTONS

Paterna Persian Yarn
260   703
604

DMC Stranded Cotton
436 Tan

DMC Perle 5
310 Black

Watercolours by Caron
Autumn Leaves

Silk ribbon YLI 4mm, 50cm (19 1/2") of each colour
159 Dark Dusty Pink
75 Dark Green
184 Dark Blue
163 Dusty Pink

Novelty buttons, 6 of each colour to match silk ribbon bows
(Note: Do not use buttons for babies as they are a safety hazard.)

Note: each length of Watercolours by Caron thread divides into 3 strands

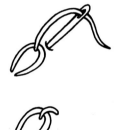

fig. 1

fig. 2

EMBROIDERY INSTRUCTIONS

All embroidery is worked with a single strand unless otherwise stated.

Gingerbread men

With 2 strands of DMC Stranded 436, appliqué the gingerbread men in place on the blanket, using a small blanket stitch around the outside edge. This will cover the tacking stitches. In DMC Perle 310, stitch French knots for the eyes and small straight stitches for the mouth, finishing with French knots at the corners of the mouth (Fig. 2). Six mouths should be smiling and two mouths should be sad.

Baskets

With 1 strand of Autumn Leaves, chain stitch around the outside and the top of the basket. Fill in the basket with trellis stitch, using the same thread.

Joining the baskets Stitch French knots with 1 strand of Autumn Leaves to join the gingerbread men to the baskets.

enlarge tracing guide by 150%

See enlargement
guide page 174

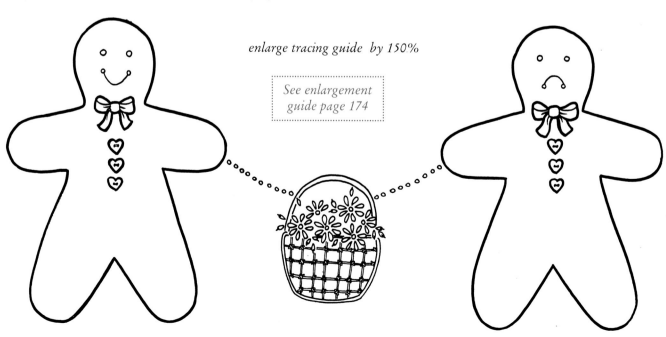

Daisies

For the petals of the daisies, stitch 6 or 7 lazy daisy stitches, radiating out from the centre, in Paterna 260. With Paterna 703 stitch a single French knot in the centre of each daisy. Stitch the leaves in lazy daisy stitches in Paterna 604. Leave a small tail on an angle at the tip of each leaf, to create movement in the leaves (Fig. 3).

Bow

Take a stitch with the silk ribbon, going in at one side of the neck of the gingerbread man and coming out at the other (Fig. 4). Tie the two tails of the ribbon and pull tightly. This will puff up the cheeks of the gingerbread man. With a matching sewing thread, take a stitch up through the middle of the knot and oversew the ribbon knot in place. This is to prevent the ribbon coming undone and being swallowed by a baby. For safety reasons, I do not recommend buttons if the blanket is to be used for a baby.

Instead, I suggest that you stitch colonial knots in Autumn Leaves, using all three strands, or use thread to match the ribbons.

fig. 3

CONSTRUCTION

Place the backing fabric face down on a table, then place the embroidered blanket right side up on top, leaving a 10cm (4") overhang of the backing fabric all the way around the blanket. Pin in place. Fold the corners over, the same way you would if you were covering a book, at a 45° angle (Fig. 5). Fold the sides over and turn under 5cm (2") so that you have a 5cm (2") border on the front of the blanket. Pin in place. Trim away any material showing on the corners, so that there is a mitred edge. Hand-stitch the backing in place with a small slip stitch (Fig. 6). Using 1 strand of Autumn Leaves, chain stitch around the edge where the fabric meets the blanket.

With the extra felt you could make a little stuffed gingerbread man to go with the blanket.

←*blanket edge*

↖*fold line*

fig. 4

↑ *chain stitch*

↖ *cut away*

←*hand stitch*

fig. 5

Little Boy Blue

ittle boy blue came about because I had many requests for a blanket for little boys. This was a pleasure to stitch, as I was able to add quirky little touches to the design, such as the mushrooms for the sheep to eat as if they aren't fat enough! The corn had to be sweet corn of course (artistic licence). The cow eating the flowers is very cute, and where would we be without the cheeky little Willie Wagtail?

Individual sections of this design would look lovely stitched on clothing or smaller projects. You could stitch this design across the blanket instead of around the outside.

The meadow. The...

The... The meadow...

cow's in the corn.

the sheep's in

come blow up your horn

...Little... Boy... Blue...

A

B

See enlargement
guide page 174

C

D

E

enlarge tracing guides by 200%

the meadow

the

the

cows in the

corn.

F

G

H

I

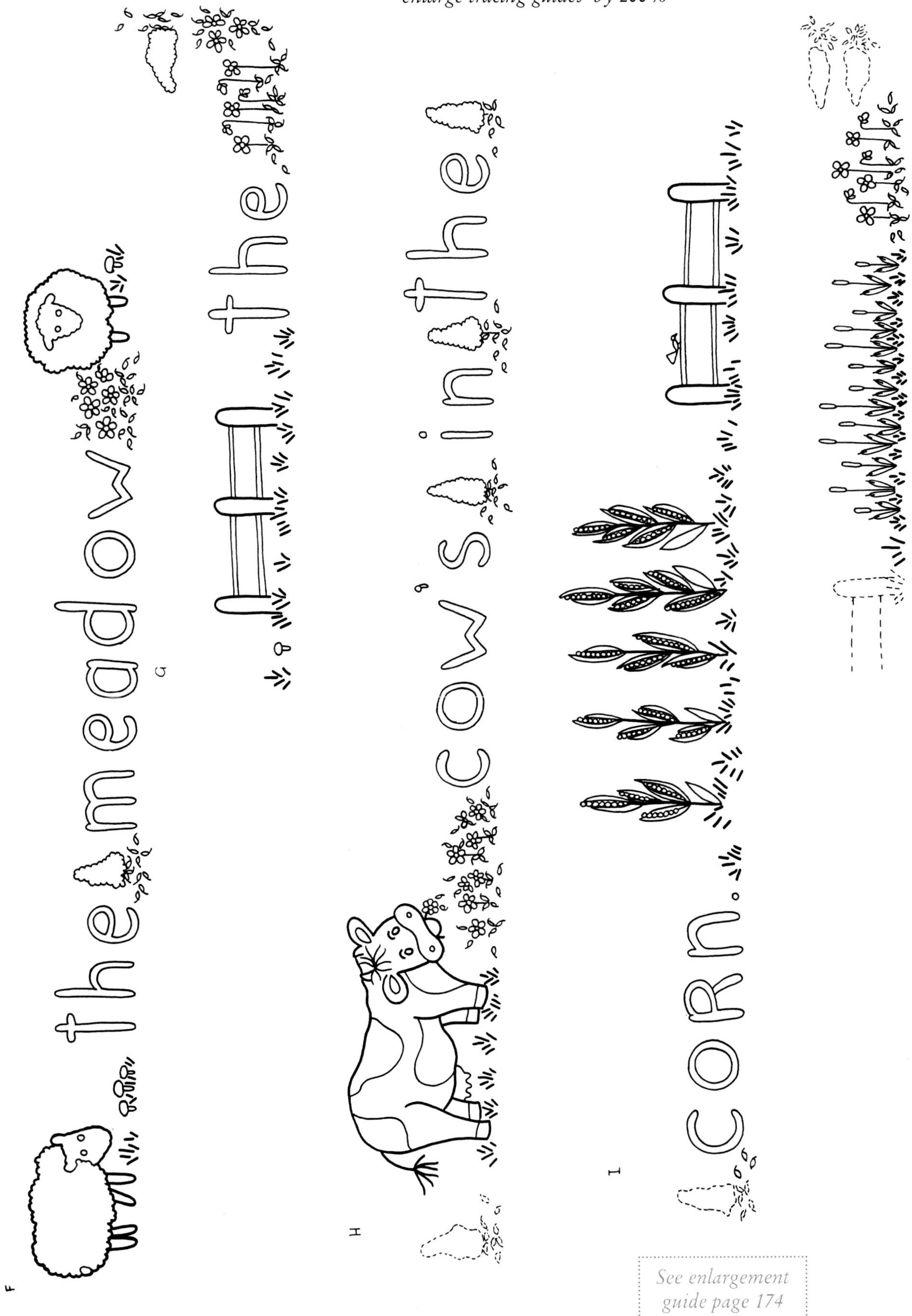

See enlargement guide page 174

THREADS

Gumnut Tulips Mohair

073	645
074	646
295	708
297	744
346	746
348	827
349	829
547	966
587	990
626	999
628	

Gumnut Buds Silk

865	998
966	
969	

DMC Perle 5
White

Watercolours by Caron
Flagstone

STITCHES

Back stitch

Whipped back stitch

Bullion stitch

Chain stitch

Fly stitch

French knot

Granitos stitch

Lazy daisy stitch

Satin stitch

Split stitch

Stem stitch

Surface stem stitch

Straight stitch

Turkey stitch

REQUIREMENTS

Cream wool blanketing, 1.1m x 80cm (43" x 31 1/4")

Printed fabric, 1.3m x 1.15m (50 3/4" x 45")

Piping, 3.8m (12' 6")

Crewel needles, No. 6 (wool thread), No. 8 (silk thread)

Straw needle No. 7 (bullions)

Water-soluble pen

Hoop, 15cm (6")

PREPARATION

TRun a large tacking thread 7cm to 10cm (2 3/4" to 4") in from the edge of the blanket. Trace the design onto tissue paper. Pin the design in place around the outside of the blanket along the tacking line (on the inside edge). Make holes in the pattern sheet with an awl or large blunt needle and then mark the design onto the blanket with the water-soluble pen. Trace and embroider the writing first. It is advisable to mark and work one section of the flowers or design at a time as it is very difficult to follow a multitude of marks on the fabric. If you find this too hard place the traced pattern onto the design and pin in place then with a contrasting thread tack around the design so you will have a tacking line to embroider. You may use a hoop if you wish but it is not necessary.

CONSTRUCTION

Pin the piping 3cm to 4cm (1 1/8" to 1 5/8") in from the outside edge of the blanket and sew in place with a sewing machine using a zipper foot. Place the backing fabric face down on a table then place the embroidered blanket right side up on top. Pin in place (Fig. 1). Fold the corners over the same way you would if you were covering a book at a 45° angle. Fold the sides over and turn under a 4cm (1 5/8") border onto the front of the blanket. Pin in place (Fig. 2). Trim away any material showing on the corners so that there is a mitred edge. Hand-stitch the backing fabric in place (Fig. 3).

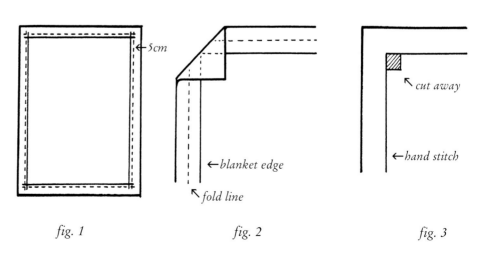

fig. 1   *fig. 2*   *fig. 3*

EMBROIDERY INSTRUCTIONS

All threads are single strand unless otherwise stated. Stitch all the writing in chain stitch with Watercolours Flagstone.

Little Boy Blue

Hat Back stitch around the outline of the hat in Watercolours Flagstone. Fill in the crown of the hat with trellis stitch in Watercolours Flagstone then whip the back stitch around the outline of the crown in the same colour. Fill in the rim of the hat with surface stem stitch in Watercolours Flagstone.

Shirt Fill in the shirt with very densely packed split stitch in Gumnut Tulips 346 (Light Blue). Create the shading by stitching over the shirt in Gumnut Tulips 348 (Medium Blue) in straight stitch. Fill in the collar and cuffs with satin stitch in Gumnut Tulips 349 (Dark Blue) and stitch a few straight stitches in the crevices of the shirt in the same colour. Back stitch around the outline of the shirt in Gumnut Tulips 349.

Pants Fill in the pants with split stitch in Gumnut Tulips 348 then create shading by stitching straight stitches over the pants in Gumnut Tulips 349. Back stitch around the outline of the pants in Gumnut Tulips 349.

Belt gloves and boots Stitch the belt in chain stitch in Gumnut Buds 969. Fill in the gloves and boots with satin stitch in the same colour.

Sheep

Fill in the head of the sheep with French knots in Gumnut Buds 998 and Gumnut Tulips 999 threaded in the needle together. Using the same colour stitch 2 straight stitches for each leg then stitch a fly stitch with the point facing out for the tail. Stitch the body of the sheep in French knots in Gumnut Tulips 990 and DMC Perle (White) threaded in the needle together. Stitch French knots for the eyes in the same colour.

Cow

Stitch back stitch around the outlines of the cow in Gumnut Buds 998. Back stitch around the nose and udder in Gumnut Buds 865. Fill in the black areas on the cow with split stitch in Gumnut Tulips 999 packing the stitches very close together. Fill in the body of the cow with split stitch in Gumnut Tulips 990 packing the stitches very close together. Stitch the tail in chain stitch in Gumnut Buds 998 then stitch 4 turkey stitches for the tail tuft. Satin stitch the eyes with Gumnut Buds 998 then stitch straight stitches for the eyebrows. With the same colour stitch some straight stitches at the top of the head. Finish with some turkey stitches for the tuft of hair at the top of the cow's head. Fill in the nose the inside of the ears and the udder with satin stitch in Gumnut Buds 865. Stitch the nostril holes with French knots in Gumnut Buds 998.

Dandelions

Stitch the petals of the flowers in lazy daisy stitch in Gumnut Tulips 708. Stitch the leaves in Gumnut Tulips 628 in lazy daisy stitch then stitch a French knot in the centre of each flower in Gumnut Buds 969.

Lupins

Fill in the flower heads with French knots in Gumnut Tulips 074 (Dark Pink) 073 (Pale Pink) 297 (Dark Purple) and 295 (Light Purple). Fill each lupin with only one colour giving you four different coloured flower heads. Stitch the leaves and stems in Gumnut Tulips 547 in lazy daisy stitch for the leaves and small straight stitches for the stems.

Hay

Fill in the hay sheaves with split stitch in Gumnut Tulips 746 (Dark Gold) and 744 (Medium Gold). Stitch the colours over each other as this will give a nice texture to the hay. Tie off the top of the hay with some straight stitches and a bow in Gumnut Buds 966.

Grass

Stitch straight stitches for the grass in Gumnut Tulips 645/646.

Wheat

Stitch a 5-wrap bullion stitch for the wheat heads in Gumnut Tulips 744. With the same colour stem stitch the stem and stitch long lazy daisy stitches with a long tail for the leaves.

Mushrooms

Fill in the heads of the mushrooms with satin stitch in Gumnut Buds 966. With the same colour work 3 straight stitches stitched closely together for the stems.

Poppies

The poppies are stitched using 2 colours working each flower in a single colour and alternating the colours to create shading. Fill in the petals and buds of the flowers with Granitos stitch in Gumnut Tulips 829 (Dark Red) and 827 (Medium Red). Stitch a single French knot in the centre of the flowers with Gumnut Buds 998. With Gumnut Tulips 626 stem stitch the stems and stitch lazy daisy stitches for the leaves. At the top of the bud stitch 2 straight stitches on either side of the bud.

Fence

Fill in the fence posts with satin stitch in Gumnut Tulips 966. Don't make the posts too straight as fence posts are uneven. Stitch the wire in stem stitch in the same colour.

Willy Wagtail

With Gumnut Tulips 999 stitch the body of the Willy Wagtail with a Granitos stitch then satin stitch the tail and head. Stitch small straight stitches for the legs and beak.

Corn

Stem stitch the stems of the corn in Gumnut Tulips 587. The corn cob is created by stitching the cob in French knots with Gumnut Tulips 708. Stitch long straight stitches on either side of the cob in Gumnut Tulips 587. Finish with straight stitch grass in the same colour.

Horn

With Gumnut Buds 746 fill in the horn with satin stitch and stitch back stitch around the horn rim. Tie a red bow in silk ribbon YLI No. 3 or any other colour of your choice around the horn.

Embroidered Hearts
receiving blanket

This is a great project to stitch for yourself or a loved one. You can stitch one heart at a time so it is a good way to introduce yourself to new stitches and ways of using the techniques. The individual hearts would look attractive embroidered on a cushion, a hot water bottle cover, in the corner of a blanket or on a capsule rug for a baby.

Or you could stitch the designs across the top of a large blanket, then fold the blanket back over the sheet, which would look stunning as we are starting to see more wool blanketing and embroidery used in home decorating. If this design is being stitched for an adult you may like to add beads to the flowers in the design, and pearls between the French knots on the heart. The beads catch the light and add a richness to the work.

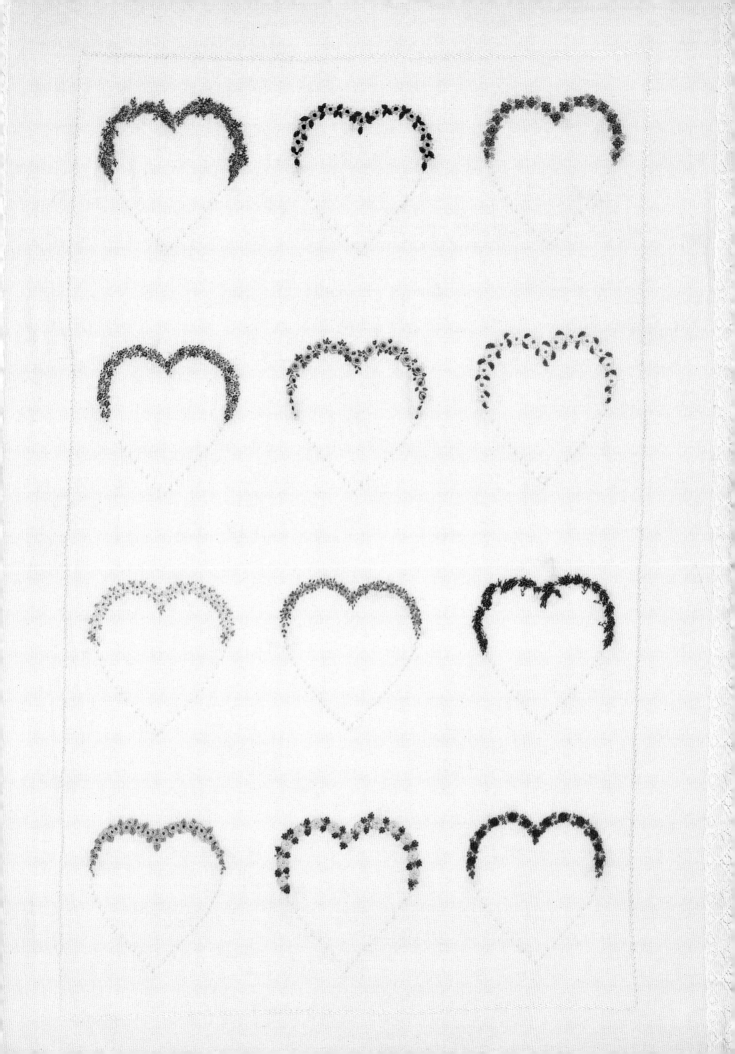

THREADS

**Appletons
Crewel Wool**

141	642
143	643
292	693
341	741
343	751
351	754
352	872
472	877
473	884
505	885
542	886
552	992
603	

Anchor Marlitt

800	898
816	1019
817	1078
868	1207
895	1212

*DMC Broder
Medicis Wool*

8027	8405

*Paterna
Persian Yarn*

260

STITCHES

Blanket stitch
Bullion stitch
Colonial knot
Feather stitch
Fly stitch
French knot
Lazy daisy stitch
Pistil stitch
Satin stitch
Spider stitch
Straight stitch
*Raised
straight stitch*

REQUIREMENTS

Cream wool flannel, 1.1m x 70cm (43" x 27 1/4")

Lightweight wool mix backing fabric, 1.2m x 80cm (46 7/8"x 31 1/4")

Cream cotton lace, 4.3m x 6cm (14' x 2 3/8")

Chenille needle Nos 22, 24 (wool thread)

Crewel needles, No. 6 (wool thread), No. 9 (rayon thread)

Straw needle No. 7 (bullions)

Cable or knitting needle

Hoop, 20cm (8")

Water-soluble pen

PLACEMENT OF DESIGNS

Run a large tacking thread down the middle and across the centre of the wool fabric to mark the centre of the blanket. Mark the fabric into rectangles from the centre, 20cm (8") across by 25cm (9 3/4") down. You should end up with 12 rectangles (Fig. 1). Cut a heart template from Templastic. To centre the heart draw a cross in each rectangle and place the heart template in position. When you are happy with the placement, trace the cross onto the heart (Fig. 2) and then trace around the heart outline onto the wool with the water-soluble pen. The cross on the template will allow you to align the designs in all the rectangles.

llustrations for this blanket should be enlarged. An enlargement guide for photocopying is on page 174.

enlarge template by 150%

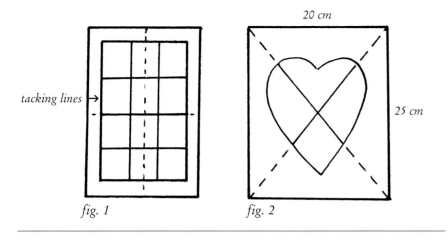

tacking lines →

20 cm

25 cm

fig. 1

fig. 2

CONSTRUCTION

Place the backing fabric face down on a table then place the embroidered blanket right side up on top. Pin in place (Fig. 1). Fold the fabric over 2.4cm (1") and then fold the corners over the same way you would if you were covering a book at a 45° angle (Fig. 2). Fold the sides over and turn under 1.2cm (¹/₂") so that you have a 1.2cm (¹/₂") border on the front of the blanket. Pin in place. Trim away any material showing on the corners so that there is a mitred edge (Fig. 3). Hand-stitch the backing to the blanketing then pin the lace onto the blanketing so that it covers the backing fabric. Hand-stitch in place. Mitre the corners of the lace and run a small running stitch to hold them together then stitch a very small blanket stitch on the back of the lace join.

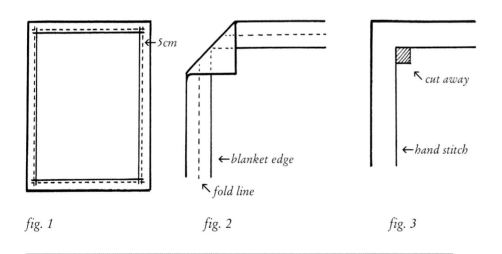

←5cm

←blanket edge

↖fold line

↖cut away

←hand stitch

fig. 1

fig. 2

fig. 3

EMBROIDERY INSTRUCTIONS

All embroidery is worked with a single strand unless otherwise stated.

Border Stitch around the outside edge of the large rectangle surrounding all the hearts in feather stitch with 2 strands of Marlitt 1212.

Hearts With Appletons 992 and Marlitt 1212 threaded together in the same needle stitch colonial knots around the lower portion of all the hearts.

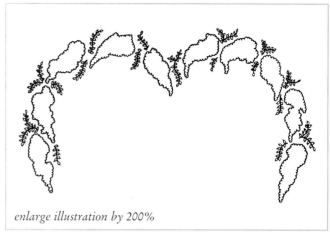

enlarge illustration by 200%

fig. 1   fig. 2

Heart No. 1 ~ Wisteria

Fill in the flower heads with French knots using Appletons 741 for some heads and Appletons 886 for the rest to create shading (Fig. 1). Stem stitch the stems in Appletons 343. Stitch lazy daisy stitch for the leaves in the same colour. Add small lazy daisy stitch highlights in Marlitt 895 between the leaves (Fig. 2).

enlarge illustration by 200%

fig. 3

Heart No. 2 ~ Sunflowers

With Appletons 472 stitch 7 to 14 lazy daisy petals for each flower. Leave a small circle in the centre of the flower and work 5 to 6 French knots in the space with Appletons 505. Stitch the leaves in Appletons 643 in satin stitch worked on a slight angle. Stitch down one side and then the other slanting the stitches into the centre vein (Fig. 3).

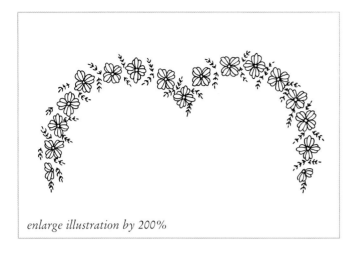

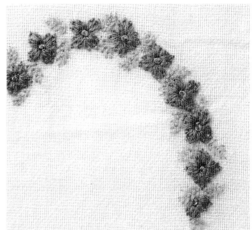

Heart No. 3 ~ Pink star flowers

With Appletons 141 stitch 3 lazy daisy stitches for each petal making the centre lazy daisy stitch longer than the other 2 (Fig. 4). Stitch a single French knot in Appletons 693 and Marlitt 868 threaded in the same needle together. For the leaves stitch very small fly stitches on a slight curve in Appletons 351. Stitch a straight stitch at the tip of each leaf (Fig. 5).

fig. 4   *fig. 5*

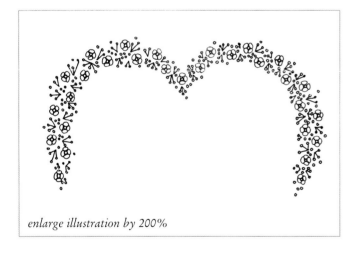

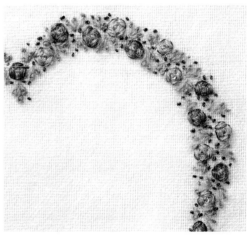

Heart No. 4 ~ Mauve flowers

With Appletons 885 stitch 3 very small straight stitches for each petal coming up at A going down at B and coming up at A. Lay the thread to the right of the middle stitch and go down at B and come up at A then lay the thread to the left of the middle stitch and go down at B (Fig. 6). With Marlitt 817 stitch a small straight stitch around the outside of the petals coming up at A and going down at B (Fig. 7). Repeat the above steps for the second flower using Appletons 884 and Marlitt 816. This way you will have alternating medium and pale mauve flowers. The centre is stitched with a single French knot in Appletons 472 and Marlitt 1078 threaded together in the same needle. The leaves are stitched in small pistil stitches in Appletons 542. Between the flowers scatter French knots in Marlitt 817.

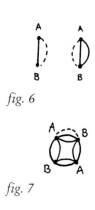

fig. 6

fig. 7

enlarge illustration by 200%

Heart No. 5 ~ Roses

The roses are stitched in the combinations below in bullion stitch:
Centre of rose Appletons 754 with 2 x 7-wrap bullions; *Middle petals* Appletons 751 with 4 x 9-wrap bullions; *Outer petals* Appletons 877 with 11 x 11-wrap bullions

fig. 8

The large rose buds are stitched in the combinations below in bullion stitch:
Centre of the bud Appletons 754 with 2 x 7-wrap bullions;
Middle of the bud Appletons 751 with 2 x 9-wrap bullions stitched 1 on each side of the centre bullions; *Outer petals* Appletons 877 with 2 x 11-wrap bullions on the outside of the bud; *Calyx* fly stitch in Appletons 642 (Fig. 8)

For the small buds mix Appletons 754 and 751 in the needle together and stitch a single French knot for each bud. Stitch a very small fly stitch around each small bud in Appletons 642 for the calyx (Fig. 8). Fill in between the roses and buds with lazy daisy stitches for the leaves in Appletons 642 then add some French knots scattered throughout the design in the same colour.

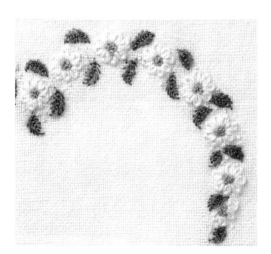

enlarge illustration by 200%

Heart No. 6 ~ Shasta daisies

Stitch 7 to 8 lazy daisy stitch petals for each flower in Paterna 260. At the centre of each flower stitch 5 to 6 French knots in Appletons 473. The leaves are stitched in Appletons 292 with a very small close fly stitch stitched on a slight angle (Fig. 9). Scatter French knots in Marlitt 800 between the flowers to create highlights.

fig. 9

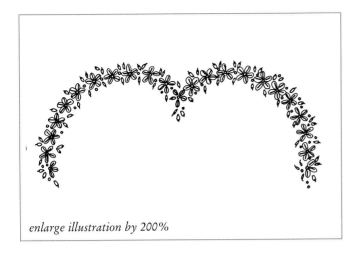

enlarge illustration by 200%

Heart No. 7 ~ Yellow daisies

Stitch 5 lazy daisy stitch petals to each flower with
Appletons 872. Add a straight stitch to the centre of each
petal in Medicis 8027 (Fig. 10). Thread Medicis 8405 and
Marlitt 1078 in the same needle and stitch a single French
knot for the centre of each flower. Stitch the leaves with
lazy daisy stitches in Appletons 352 and then scatter
French knots throughout the design in the same colour.

fig. 10

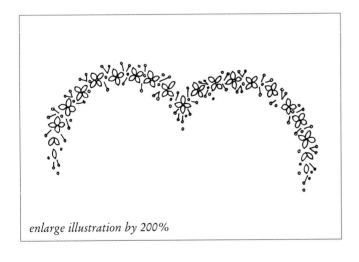

enlarge illustration by 200%

Heart No. 8 — Cornflowers

The 4 flower petals are worked by mixing Appletons 886
and 741 together in the same needle and stitching 3 small
straight stitches for each petal (Fig. 6). For the leaves stitch
small groups of pistil stitches in Appletons 292 then
scatter French knots throughout the design in the same
colour.

fig. 6

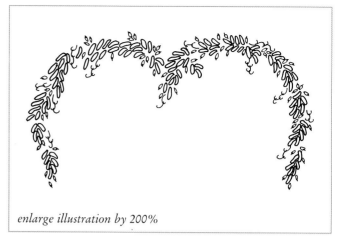

enlarge illustration by 200%

Heart No. 9 ~ Lavender

The lavender flower heads are stitched in an 11-wrap bullion stitch in Appletons 603.

Try to make the flower heads with a slight loop by picking up a smaller amount of fabric than the length of the bullion. With Appletons 642 stitch a mixture of fly stitch and lazy daisy stitch leaves randomly.

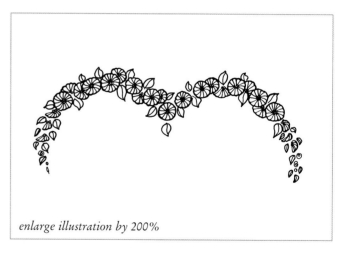

enlarge illustration by 200%

fig. 11

fig. 3

Heart No. 10 ~ Hollyhocks

With Appletons 751 fill in the flowers with blanket stitch. For the buds stitch a half blanket stitch in Appletons 751 (Fig. 11). Stitch French knots at the very tip of the swag in the same colour. Fill in the centres of the flowers with French knots in Marlitt 1207. Fill in the leaves with Appletons 351 in satin stitch worked on a slight angle. Stitch down one side and then the other sloping the stitches into the centre vein (see Fig. 3).

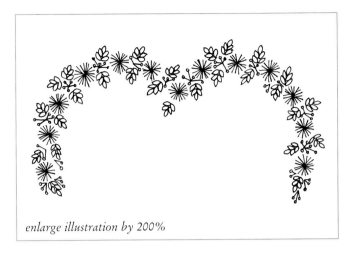

enlarge illustration by 200%

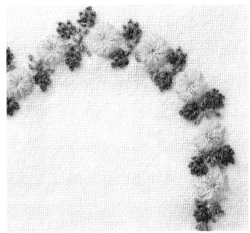

Heart No. 11 ~ Chrysanthemums

The petals of the flowers are first stitched with raised straight stitch in Appletons 552. Then with Marlitt 898 stitch a raised straight stitch between the first row of petals (Fig. 12). Raised straight stitch should sit up loosely off the fabric. Use a cable needle to hold the thread up from the fabric as you pull it through. Stitch 5 lazy daisy stitch petals for the leaves grouped very closely together in Appletons 292. Fill in between in Appletons 341 with small pistil stitches.

fig. 12

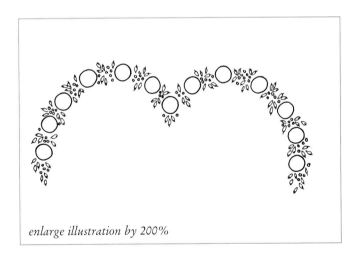

enlarge illustration by 200%

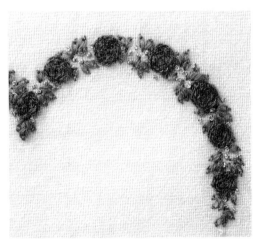

Heart No. 12 ~ Camellias

Fill in the flower heads with spider stitch in Appletons 143. The leaves are stitched in lazy daisy stitch in Appletons 292. Scatter French knots in Marlitt 1019 throughout the design to add highlights.

Morning Stroll

I have always wanted to keep geese, but if I can't have them I will stitch them. When I was stitching the design, my daughter rang from the country and said that she had a flock of visiting geese wandering through her garden on their morning stroll — hence the name of the blanket. They appeared mysteriously in the mist, strolled through and were gone again.

The geese seem to dance across the airy blue blanket in this design and the silk ribbons sparkle in the morning sun. The swag at the top would look lovely stitched on its own and framed. Or you could use different elements of this design to create smaller masterpieces on clothing, crib covers, towels or kindergarten bags, or around the bottom of a small girl's skirt.

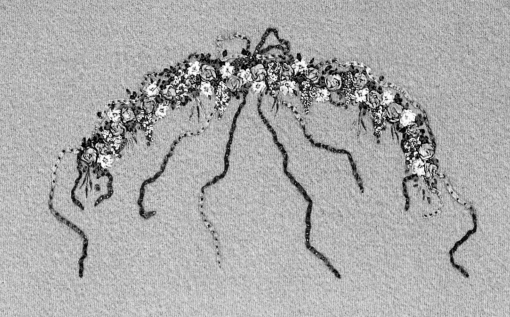

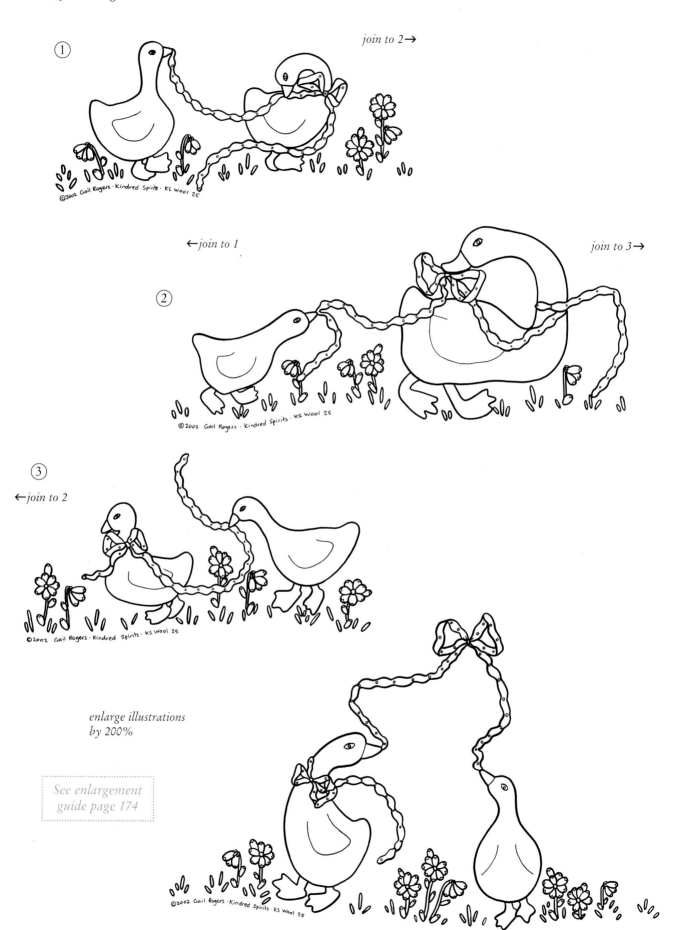

① join to 2→

←join to 1

②

join to 3→

③

←join to 2

*enlarge illustrations
by 200%*

*See enlargement
guide page 174*

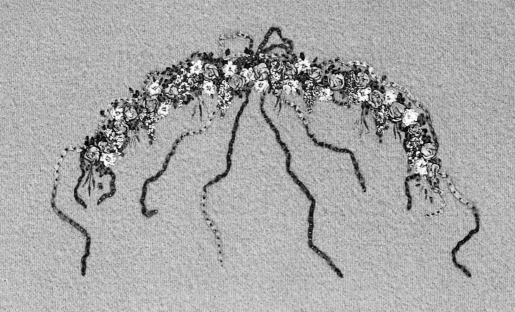

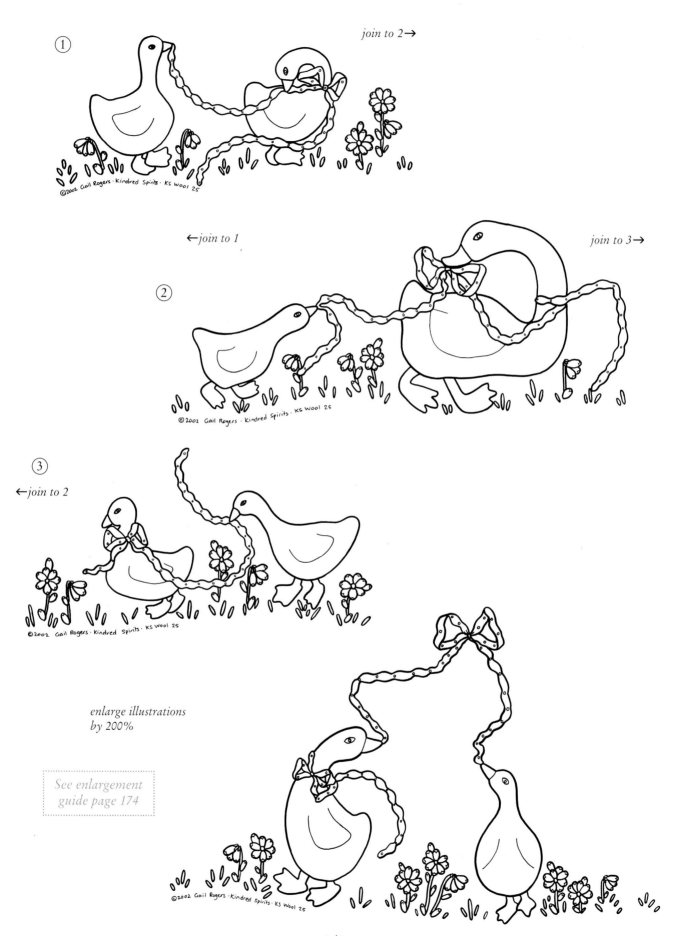

① join to 2→

←join to 1   join to 3→

②

③

←join to 2

*enlarge illustrations
by 200%*

See enlargement
guide page 174

©2002 Gail Rogers · Kindred Spirits · KS Wool 25

REQUIREMENTS

Pale blue wool blanketing, 1.1m x 80cm (43" x 31 1/4")

Printed fabric for backing, 1.3m x 1m (50 3/4" x 39")

Antique white shaggy plush felt, (I used Kunin felt),
   50cm x 30cm (19 1/2" x 11 3/4")

Orange piping, 3.8m (12' 6")

Crewel needles, No. 6 (wool threads), No. 9 (rayon threads)

Chenille needle No. 18 (silk ribbon)

Straw needle No. 7 (bullions)

Water-soluble pen

Embroidery hoop in size most comfortable to work silk ribbon

STITCHES

Blanket stitch   *Satin stitch*

Bullion stitch   *Stem stitch*

French knot   *Straight stitch*

Ribbon stitch

CONSTRUCTION OF THE FINISHED BLANKET
Refer to page 174 for instructions.

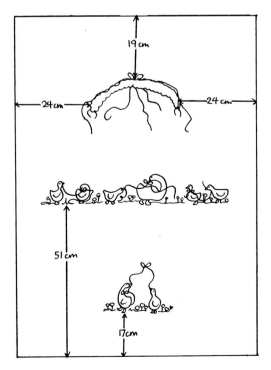

EMBROIDERY INSTRUCTIONS

Run a large tacking thread down the middle and across the centre of the wool fabric to mark the centre of the blanket. It is advisable to mark and work one section of the flowers or design at a time, as it is very difficult to follow a multitude of marks on this fabric.

All embroidery is done with a single strand unless otherwise stated.

llustrations for this blanket should be enlarged. See page 174 for enlargement guide.

THREADS & RIBBONS

Colour Streams Silk Ribbon

No. 1 Wisteria, 4mm (3/16")
No. 2 Water Nymphs, 4mm (3/16")
No. 13 Mulberry Blues, 4mm (3/16") (2 packets)
No. 18 Antique Ivory, 4mm (3/16") (2 packets)
No. 26 Exotic Lights Tuscan Olive, 4mm (3/16")
No. 30 Eucalypt, 4mm (3/16")
No. 23 Rose Blush, 7mm (1/4") (2 packets)
No. 25 Umbrian Gold, 7mm (1/4")

DMC Rayon
30746

Colour Streams Silk Thread

No. 4 Exotic Lights Straw
No. 13 Ophir Mulberry Blues
No. 26 Exotic Lights Tuscan Olive

Gumnut Silk Buds
788   *998*

Geese

Trace the geese from the pattern sheet onto paper or Templastic and cut them out. Pin the geese shapes to the felt. Cut the geese out of the felt, making sure that the loops on the felt all run in the same direction. Pin the geese in place on the blanket, using the photo and design layout as a guide, remembering that the backing fabric folds over 5cm (2") all around the blanket. Tack the geese in place, stitching very close to the outside edge of each goose, then blanket stitch around the outside edge of the geese with 2 strands of DMC 30746, making sure that the stitches are small and even. Stem stitch the lines for the wings with 2 strands of DMC 30746. Take every third stitch through to the back of the blanket, using a stabbing motion, to give the goose shape.

With Gumnut Buds 998 back stitch the outline of the eye, then stitch a single French knot in the centre, to highlight the eye. With Gumnut Buds 788, fill in the beak and feet with satin stitch.

fig. 1

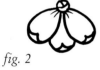

fig. 2

fig. 3

Daisies

The daisies are stitched in ribbon stitch in Colour Streams 4mm (³/₁₆") Antique Ivory. Stitch a single French knot in the centre of each flower in Colour Streams Exotic Lights Straw. With Exotic Lights Tuscan Olive, stitch straight stitches for the stem and grass. For the buds, stitch 3 small straight stitches at the top of the stem, going in the same hole at the stem and spreading out to the petals.

The leaves are stitched in ribbon stitch with Colour Streams 4mm (³/₁₆")Tuscan Olive and Eucalypt. Stitch the leaves randomly up the stem and around the flower, using both colours for each flower to create shading. Catch the stems in place with the leaves by coming up in the stem with the ribbon. This will anchor the stem in place.

Ribbons

Tie a bow in Colour Streams 4mm (³/₁₆") Mulberry Blues, leaving long ends to pin in place on the blanket where indicated on the pattern sheet. Thread the ribbon in the needle and take the ends through to the back of the blanket. Secure the ribbon at the back of the blanket with a matching thread. Anchor the ribbon on the front of the blanket with French knots in Colour Streams Ophir Mulberry Blues. Use this method for all the ribbons.

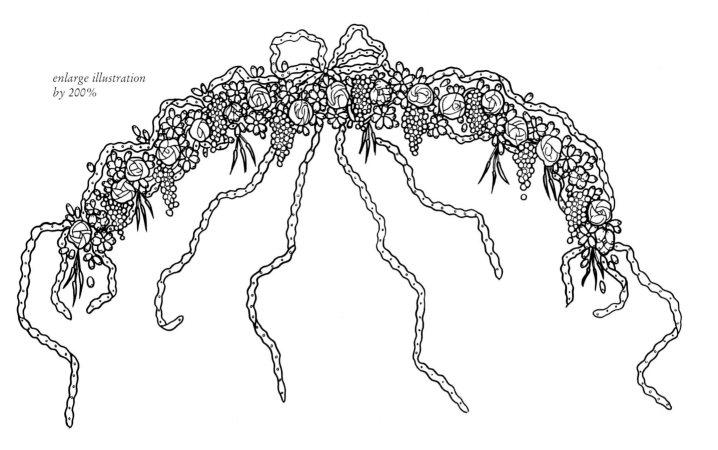

enlarge illustration by 200%

Swag roses

Stitch a French knot in Colour Streams 7mm ($^1/_4$") Umbrian Gold for the centre of the roses. Stem stitch around the centre twice in Colour Streams 7mm ($^1/_4$") Rose Blush, to create the rose petals. For the buds, stitch a French knot in Colour Streams 7mm ($^1/_4$") Umbrian Gold, then stitch ribbon stitches over the French knot in Colour Streams 7mm ($^1/_4$") Rose Blush to form the bud.

Swag daisies

The daisies are stitched with ribbon stitch in Colour Streams 4mm ($^3/_{16}$") Antique Ivory. Stitch a single French knot in the centre in Colour Streams Exotic Lights Straw.

Swag wisteria

Stitch French knots in Colour Streams 4mm ($^3/_{16}$") Wisteria and Water Nymphs. Blend the two shades together to give variation to the clusters.

Swag leaves

The leaves are stitched in ribbon stitch with Colour Streams 4mm ($^3/_{16}$") Tuscan Olive and Eucalypt stitched randomly throughout the swag design to create shading.

Swag bullion clusters

Stitch 15-wrap bullions for the cluster heads in Colour Streams Ophir Mulberry Blues. Stitch a small straight stitch at the end of each bullion, then stitch a long straight stitch leg to join the bullion to the swag, in the same colour.

Heart's Desire
baby blanket

Wrap your newborn baby in this delicate blanket, stitched with love. There is more work in this design, but the soft pastel colours make it a favourite for newborn babies. It would be nice to stitch one section of this design on the bumper pad at the end of baby's cot, or on any other accessories for baby, such as a nappy holder. Please exercise caution with the bumper pad and make sure that it has many ties to secure it firmly so that it will not come loose and fall on baby's face.

REQUIREMENTS

Cream wool blanketing, 1.1m x 80cm (43" x 31 1/4")

Plain cream backing fabric, 1.3m x 1m (50 3/4" x 39")

Cream piping, 3.8m (12' 6")

Chenille needles, Nos 22, 24 (wool thread)

Crewel needle No. 6 (Perle cotton)

3.8m (12' 6") cream piping

Water-soluble pen

Hoop, 20cm (8") (for trellis stitch)

THREADS

*Watercolours
by Caron
Faded Linen*

*Gumnut Yarns
Gemstones*

A1	GR1
B2	J2

*Gumnut Yarns
Blossoms*

191	642
232	742
294	743
383	851

DMC Perle no. 5

353	818
503	819
644	3042
745	

PLACEMENT AND ORDER OF WORKING

Run a large tacking thread down the middle and across the centre of the wool blanket to mark the centre. Place the design of the heart, ribbons and flowers in each corner of the blanket. The point of the heart should be 20cm (8") from each side of the blanket and 28cm (11") from the corner (Fig. 1). Pin the pattern in place. Make holes in the pattern sheet and mark dots on the blanket where the design goes with a water-soluble pen. I suggest that you mark and embroider the hearts and ribbons first, then mark and embroider one type of flower at a time because it is very difficult to follow a multitude of marks on wool. When the hearts are embroidered, place the small flower design 20cm (8") from the edge of the blanket and halfway between the hearts, on each long side of the blanket. Pin the pattern in place and mark dots on the blanket where the design goes with a water-soluble pen. Complete the embroidery.

STITCHES

Fly stitch

French knot

Lazy daisy stitch

Satin stitch

Padded satin stitch

Stem stitch

Straight stitch

Trellis stitch

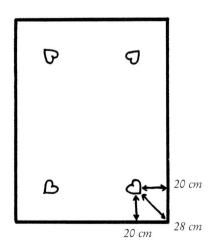

20 cm

20 cm   28 cm

CONSTRUCTION OF THE FINISHED BLANKET

Refer to page 174 for instructions.

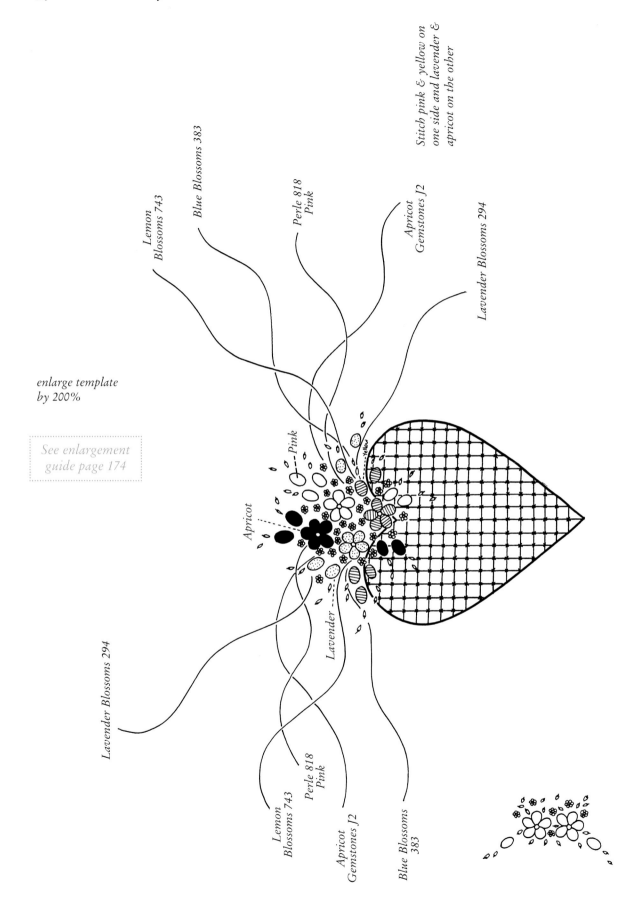

Lemon
Blossoms 743

Blue Blossoms 383

Perle 818
Pink

Apricot
Gemstones J2

Stitch pink & yellow on
one side and lavender &
apricot on the other

Lavender Blossoms 294

enlarge template
by 200%

See enlargement
guide page 174

Pink

Apricot

Lavender

Lavender Blossoms 294

Lemon
Blossoms 743

Perle 818
Pink

Apricot
Gemstones J2

Blue Blossoms
383

EMBROIDERY INSTRUCTIONS

All embroidery is worked with a single strand unless otherwise stated.

Heart

Fill in the heart with trellis stitch in Watercolours Faded Linen. Using the same colour stitch around the outline of the heart in chain stitch.

Ribbons

Stitch the ribbons in stem stitch referring to the design for colour placement. Colours used are Blossoms 294, 383 and 743 Gemstones J2 and DMC Perle 818.

Stitches for flowers other than forget-me-nots

The same embroidery stitches are used for all flowers other than the forget-me-nots. The instructions are given below followed by the thread colours for each. Forget-me-nots are the last flowers to be embroidered.

Flowers Petals are stitched with padded satin stitch. Start at the base of the petal coming up at A and going down at B (Fig. 1). For the next stitch come up at A lay the thread to the right of the first stitch and go down at B (Fig. 2). Next come up at A lay the thread to the left of the first straight stitch and go down at B (Fig. 3). Repeat this procedure 3 times. Complete all 5 petals in this way.

Flower highlights Work a fly stitch at the tip of each petal (Fig. 4). Stitch a straight stitch coming up at A and going down at B (Fig. 5).

Flower centre This is made with a single French knot using DMC Perle 745 and DMC Perle 644 threaded together in the needle.

Buds The buds are stitched with a padded satin stitch. Start at the base of the bud coming up at A and going down at B (Fig. 1). For the next stitch come up at A lay the thread to the right of the first stitch and go down at B (Fig. 2). Next come up at A lay the thread to the left of the first straight stitch and go down at B (Fig. 3). Repeat this procedure 3 times.

Bud highlights Stitch a fly stitch at the tip of each petal (Fig. 4). Stitch a straight stitch coming up at A and going down at B (Fig. 5).

Leaves Stitch 2 lazy daisy stitches at the tip of each bud for the leaves. Work 2 fly stitches around the bud in the same thread making one longer than the other and then stitch a straight stitch coming up at the base of the bud and going down half-way up the bud in the same colour (Fig. 6). The inverted fly stitch is stitched early in the design as a bud highlight.

fig. 1

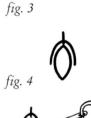

fig. 2

fig. 3

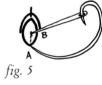

fig. 4

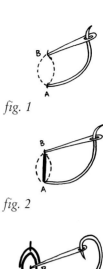

fig. 5

fig. 6

Colours for flowers other than forget-me-nots

Pale pink flowers
Petals Blossoms 191
Highlights DMC Perle 819
Centre DMC Perle 745 and 644
Bud petals Gemstones GR1
Bud highlights DMC Perle 819
Leaves Blossoms 642

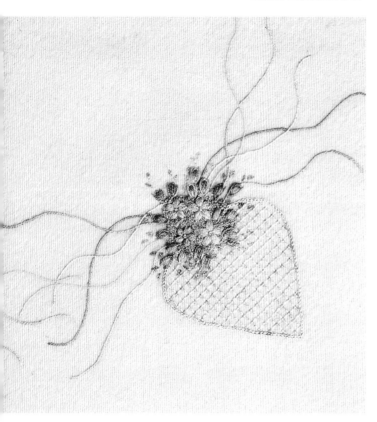

Pale lavender flowers
Petals Blossoms 232
Highlights DMC Perle 3042
Centre DMC Perle 745 and 644
Bud petals Gemstones A1
Bud highlights DMC Perle 3042
Leaves Gemstones B2

Pale apricot flowers
Petals Blossoms 851
Highlights DMC Perle 353
Centre DMC Perle 745 and 644
Bud petals Gemstones J2
Bud highlights DMC Perle 353
Leaves DMC Perle 644

Pale yellow flowers
Petals Blossoms 742
Highlights DMC Perle 745
Centre DMC Perle 745 and 644
Bud petals Blossoms 743
Bud highlights DMC Perle 745
Leaves DMC Perle 503

Forget-me-nots

Using Blossoms 383 stitch 5 French knots in a small circle. Stitch a single French knot in the centre with DMC Perle 644.

Filling stitches

To complete the design, randomly stitch some lazy daisy leaves and French, knots using the various leaf colours.

Small sprays

Stitch the designs at the sides of the blanket in the same manner as above (see design above for additional instructions).

Embroidered Wool Vest

 legant and stylish is the best way to describe this beautiful woollen vest.
This design would dress up any outfit, from jeans to a formal skirt. You may
like to stitch the design on different coloured wool for the vest or jacket.

STITCHES

Stitches

French knot

Pistil stitch

Satin stitch

Padded satin stitch

Slanted satin stitch

Stem stitch

Straight stitch

The design looks equally attractive stitched as a bell pull, or as a border on a woollen blanket. It would also look opulent stitched down the lapels of a wool dressing gown, lined with a golden yellow fabric.

REQUIREMENTS FOR VEST

Wool flannel, 70cm (27 1/4")

Backing and lining fabric of choice, 1.5m (58 1/2")

Pellon, 15cm (5 7/8")

4 covered buttons, 19mm (3/4"), or 4 pearl buttons

Vest pattern of choice

Ivory piping, 2.2m (7' 3")

Crewel needles, No. 6 (wool thread), No. 9 (rayon thread)

Chenille needles, Nos 22, 24 (wool thread)

Water-soluble pen

Hoop, 15cm (6")

Sewing threads to match both the beads and the vest fabric

ASSEMBLY INSTRUCTIONS FOR VEST

I have designed the lapel separate from the vest, so you will have to make sure that you fit the embroidered lapel to your chosen vest pattern. Trace the front vest lapel pattern and the vest pattern onto the wool flannel with a water-soluble pen. Do not cut out just yet. Make sure the lapel matches the front neck opening of your chosen vest pattern — if not, adjust to fit. Trace the embroidery pattern onto the lapel. Complete all embroidery before you cut out the fabric, or it won't fit in a hoop. Place the Pellon behind the traced lapel design and tack in place. Embroider the vest lapel according to the instructions and the design. When cutting the lapel out make sure that it fits the vest pattern, making adjustments if necessary. Also cut extra lining fabric to line the lapel. The piping is used around the front of the vest. Two buttons are stitched each side of the vest, very close together, and a blanket stitch loop is used to close the vest (see Fig. 10 on page 155).
Make up vest according to your pattern.

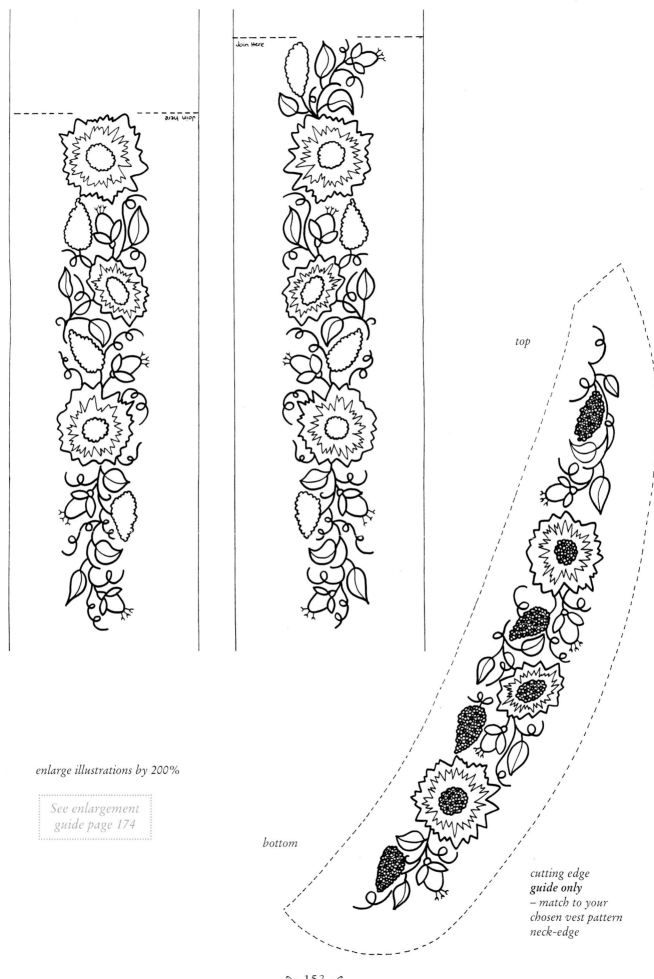

Join Here

Join Here

top

enlarge illustrations by 200%

*See enlargement
guide page 174*

bottom

cutting edge
guide only
– match to your
chosen vest pattern
neck-edge

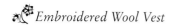

REQUIREMENTS FOR BELL PULL

Wool flannel 70cm x 15cm (27 1/4" x 5 7/8")

Backing and lining fabric of choice 115cm x 15cm (44 7/8" x 5 7/8")

Pellon 90cm x 15cm (35 1/8" x 5 7/8")

Ivory piping 1.6m (62 3/8") ivory piping

Bell pull findings

Thread bead needle

Hoop and marker requirements are the same as for the vest.

ASSEMBLY INSTRUCTIONS FOR BELL PULL

The finished size is 65cm x 10cm (25 3/8" x 4").

Trace the design onto the wool flannel. If you have trouble tracing the design onto the fabric use a light box or hold up to the light of your window. Tack the Pellon to the back of the wool flannel. Embroider the bell pull in the same manner as the vest.

To make up the bell pull sew the piping across the top bottom and sides. Make sure you overlap the piping at the corners so the cut ends will be on the inside of the bell pull. Place the backing fabric and embroidered fabric with their right sides together and sew around the edges leaving a small hole to turn the bell pull right side out. Hand-sew the bell pull findings to the bottom and top of the completed bell pull.

EMBROIDERY INSTRUCTIONS

All embroidery is done with a single strand unless otherwise stated.

Golden flowers

Stitch the inside petals close to the centre of the flower in long and short straight stitch in Blossoms 728. With Blossoms 726 stitch the outside petals in the same manner making sure that the stitches interlock to blend the two colours together. Then in Marlitt 869 stitch long and short straight stitch highlights over the petals radiating out from the centre. The centre is made up of French knots stitched randomly in Marlitt 1003 and Gemstones H5 threaded together in the same needle and French knots in Gemstones C5. Stitch the variegated gold and pale plum beads in matching sewing thread between the French knots.

Buds

The buds are filled in with a padded satin stitch in Blossoms 857. Start at the base of the bud coming up at A and going down at B (Fig. 1). For the next stitch come up at A and lay the thread to the right of the first stitch then go

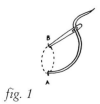

fig. 1

down at B. Next come up at A lay the thread to the left of the first straight stitch and go down at B. Repeat this procedure 4 times.

The bud highlights are stitched in Marlitt 1003 with 3 straight stitches starting at the base of the bud and going back down in the middle of the bud (Fig. 2). The centre stitch is longer than the other 2 stitches. The stamens are stitched at the tip of the bud in Marlitt 1003 with a small fly stitch (fig. 3). The sepals are stitched with a padded satin stitch in Blossoms 646. Start at the base of the bud come up at A and go down at B (Fig. 4). For the next stitch come up at A and lay the thread to the right of the first stitch. Then go down at B. Next come up at A lay the thread to the left of the first straight stitch and go down at B.

Repeat this procedure twice on the right side of the bud and then repeat for the left side of the bud (Fig. 5). Sew 3 very small straight stitches at the base of the bud (Fig. 6) to form the calyx. From the base of the bud work 3 pistil stitches in Blossoms 646 going down half-way up the bud (Fig. 7). For the highlights work 2 straight stitches in Marlitt 826 on the bud between the pistil stitches. With the same colour add straight stitch highlights on the sepals and the calyx (Fig. 8).

Leaves
The leaves are stitched in Blossoms 627 in slanted satin stitch stitched very close together.

Stems and vine
The curly vine and stems are stitched in Blossoms 645 in stem stitch.

Berries
The berries are stitched in Blossoms 198 and Gemstones GL5 in French knots in the following way. Stitch more Blossoms 198 French knots to one side of the berry (Fig. 9) then graduate the knots over to the other side of the berry. Stitch French knots in Gemstones GL5 to fill in the berry. Finish by stitching variegated plum beads with matching sewing thread randomly between the French knots on the berry.

Make up vest according to your pattern instructions (see Fig. 10 for blanket stitch loop to close the vest).

fig. 2

fig. 3

fig. 4

fig. 5

fig. 6

fig. 7

fig. 8

fig. 9

fig. 10

Resplendent as an Empress

egal, royal and rich are just a few words to describe this dazzling dressing gown. The colours, beads and metallic threads take this embroidery to a new dimension with many applications. The embroidery would look just as wonderful stitched on an evening jacket, or small sections of the design could be stitched on an evening bag or matching slippers for the gown. Elements of the design could be worked on all manners of things: a table runner, napkins and napkin rings for formal dinners, ends of scarves — or to liven up a favourite jumper.

REQUIREMENTS

Gown or jacket pattern of choice

Wool blanketing, flannel or cashmere in colour of choice
(the amount required will be shown in your pattern)

Silk lining fabric of choice, same amount as the gown
(the sample gown is completely lined)

Cottanza backing for the embroidery, 50cm (19 1/2")

Cord for piping (thickness to be determined by choice of fabric), 5 m (16' 4")

Crewel needles, No. 6 (wool thread), No. 8 (silk thread), No. 10 (Kreinik)
(or use the needle most comfortable for you)

Straw needle No. 3 (bullions)

HP pencil

Hoop, 15cm (6")

Sewing threads to match both the beads and the fabric

STITCHES

Back stitch	*French knots*
Blanket stitch	*Rope stitch*
Bullion stitch	*Satin stitch*
Chain stitch	*Padded satin stitch*
Coral stitch	*Straight stitch*
Cretan stitch	*Trellis stitch*
Fly stitch	

ASSEMBLY INSTRUCTIONS

I have designed the lapel to fit most gowns and jackets. Make a tracing of the lapel from your gown or jacket pattern and adjust the design to fit. Trace designs for the lapels, cuffs and pocket onto the silk lining with a sharp pencil. (I have used a pencil as I find that water-soluble pens tend to bleed on silk.) Do not cut out the silk until you have completed your embroidery, as the fabric will not fit into the hoop and the silk will fray. Tack the Cottanza behind the areas of silk to be embroidered.

After completing the embroidery, the piping is added — around the front opening of the gown, around the cuffs and to the pocket. Make up the gown or jacket according to your pattern.

THREADS & BEADS

The Thread Gatherer, Sheep's Silk

Chartreuse
Christmas Green
Cotton Candy DK
Fuschia
Gilded Lavender
Grape Soda
Green Leaves
Harvest Mums
Jelly Beans
Leaf Green
Marigold
Moss Green
Pumpkin Orange
Red Orange
Royalty
Seafoam Greens
Turquoise
Tutti-Frutti

Kreinik Blending Filament

021HL	028
024	034

Kreinik #4 Braid

015	154V
060	5932
102	

Kreinik #8 Braid

326

Mill Hill Petite Glass Beads

40374	42011
40556	42028

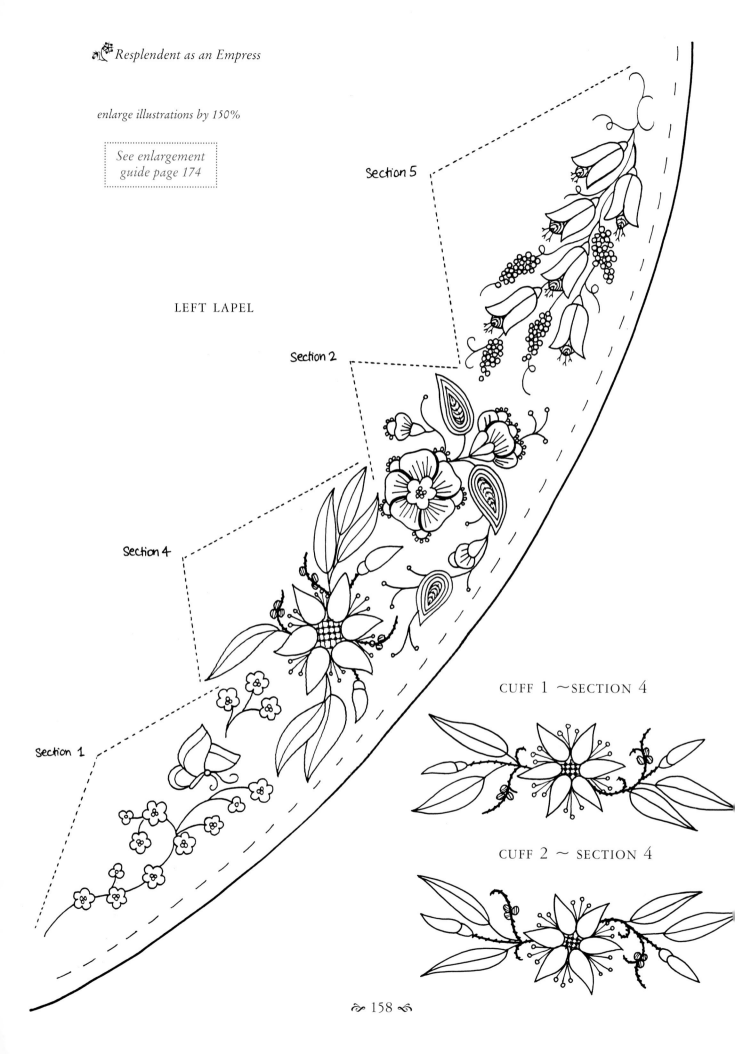

Resplendent as an Empress

enlarge illustrations by 150%

See enlargement
guide page 174

Section 5

LEFT LAPEL

Section 2

Section 4

Section 1

CUFF 1 ~ SECTION 4

CUFF 2 ~ SECTION 4

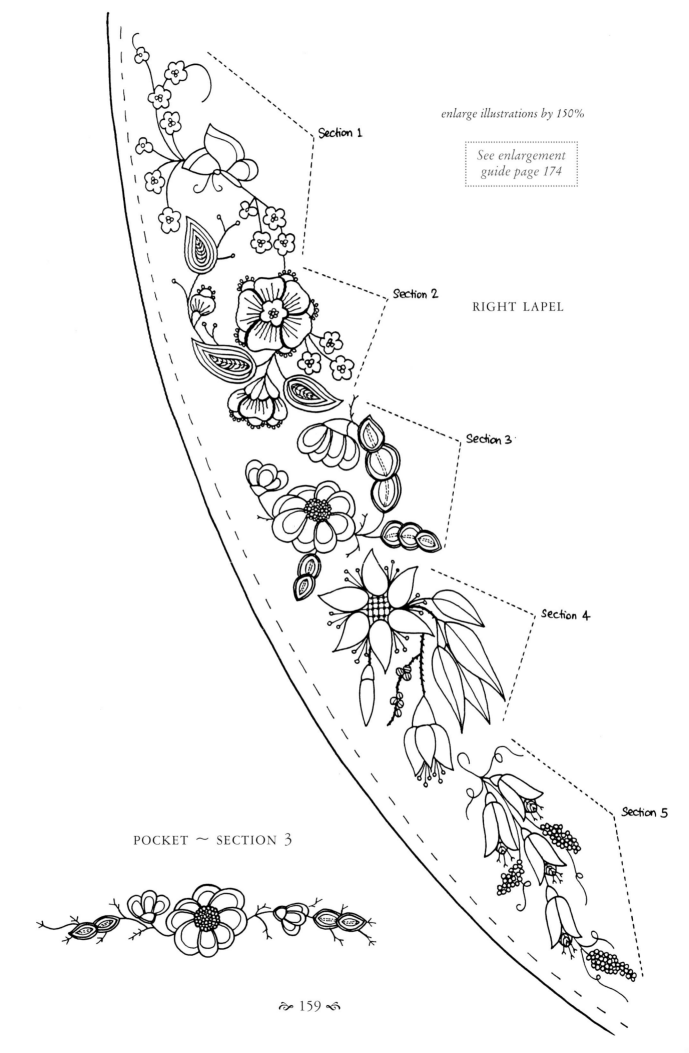

enlarge illustrations by 150%

See enlargement
guide page 174

Section 1

Section 2

RIGHT LAPEL

Section 3

Section 4

Section 5

POCKET ~ SECTION 3

EMBROIDERY INSTRUCTIONS

All embroidery is worked with a single strand unless otherwise stated.

Use a matching sewing thread to stitch the beads in place, or use a clear thread.

Section 1

Small pink flowers Fill in the petals with satin stitch in Cotton Candy DK for some of the flowers and Fuschia for the others. This will create shading. Stitch 3 beads, 42011, in the centre of each five-petal flower, and one bead in the centre of each three-petal flower. Stitch the stems in back stitch using Moss Green.

Butterfly Fill in the outside strip of the butterfly wings with blanket stitch, stitched very closely together using Pumpkin Orange. Fill in the centre wing with satin stitch, using Grape Soda and Kreinik Blending Filament (BF) 024 threaded in the needle together. Fill the two outside wings in satin stitch, using Jelly Beans and Kreinik BF 024 threaded in the needle together. Fill in the head of the butterfly with satin stitch using Kreinik #4, 154V. Using the same colour, stitch a 25-wrap bullion for the body of the butterfly. Stitch tiny back stitches in Kreinik BF 024 for the feelers.

Section 2

Large turquoise flower and buds Fill in the petals of the flower with blanket stitch in Turquoise. Highlight the petals with straight stitches using Kreinik #4, 060. With the same colour, stitch small back stitches between the petals and at the edges of the petals to create the shadows. Fill the small centre petals in with satin stitch using Marigold and Kreinik BF 028 threaded together in the needle. Stitch the small outside petals in the same colour and manner. Stitch 5 beads, 42028, in the centre and 5 of the same coloured beads around the outside edge of each of the small outside petals. Stitch the large and small buds in the same way as the large flower. Fill in the sepals of the buds with satin stitch in Green Leaves and Kreinik BF 034 threaded together in the needle.

Leaves Stitch the outside row of the leaf in chain stitch with Leaf Green, then work the second row in chain stitch with Kreinik #4, 5932. Finish with another row of chain stitch in Leaf Green, keeping the rows packed very close together. Fill in the centre of the leaf in cretan stitch with Tutti-Frutti. The stems are stitched in back stitch with Green Leaves. Stitch a single bead, 42028, at the end of each stem.

Section 3

Large orange flower and buds Fill in the outside bands of petals of the large flower with satin stitch in Red Orange. Satin stitch the centre of the petals with Harvest Mums. Fill the centre of the flower with beads, 40374, packed very tightly together. The buds are finished in the same manner as the large flower. Stitch the sepals of the buds in cretan stitch with Christmas Green, then back stitch around the outside edge of the sepal with Green Leaves.

Leaves Fill in the centre of the leaves with fly stitch in Seafoam Green. Stitch rope stitch around the edge of the fly stitch in the centre of the leaf in Christmas Green. Outline the outside edge of the leaves in back stitch in Green Leaves and back stitch the stems in the same colour. Stitch small straight stitches for the spiked stems in Kreinik #4, 102.

Section 4

Large purple flower and buds Stitch the petals in satin stitch worked on a slant in Royalty. Fill the centre of the flower with trellis stitch in Pumpkin and stitch the crosses on the trellis in Kreinik BF 021HL. Stitch the filaments radiating out from between the petals in straight stitch in the same colour, then stitch a bead, 40556, at the end of each filament. Stitch the buds in the same manner as the flower. Fill in the sepals of the buds with satin stitch in Gilded Lavender, and stitch the stems in coral stitch in the same colour. The nuts are stitched in small padded satin stitch using Pumpkin Orange and Kreinik BF 021HL threaded together in the needle. Stitch the stems in coral stitch in Gilded Lavender.

Leaves Fill the leaves with slanted satin stitch, angled into the centre vein, with Gilded Lavender. The stems of the leaves are stitched with tiny back stitches in the same colour.

Section 5

Bell Flowers Fill the outside petals of the bell flowers with satin stitch in Grape Soda. Stitch cretan stitch for the small centre petal in Jelly Beans and Kreinik BF 034 threaded together in the needle. Stitch small fly stitches hanging from the centre petal in Kreinik BF 034. Satin stitch the sepals of the flowers in Chartreuse. Back stitch the stems and tendrils in Kreinik #4, 015.

Berries Fill in the berry clusters with French knots in Fuschia and Kreinik #8, 326, threaded together in the needle.

Cuffs

The embroidery on the cuffs is stitched in the same manner as the corresponding design on the lapels.

Pocket

The embroidery on the overturn on the pocket is stitched in the same manner as the corresponding design on the lapels.

Stitch Glossary

Back Stitch

Bring the thread up just in from the start on the right side of the work. Take the needle back down and bring up a little to the left of the last stitch, then insert the needle back at the beginning of the last stitch. Repeat.

Bullion Stitch

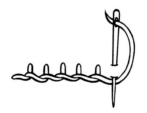

Bring the needle up through the fabric and make a small back stitch. Do not pull the needle right through. Wrap the thread around the shank of the needle the desired number of times. Hold the twisted thread with the thumb of the left hand close to the fabric. Gently pull the thread through the bullion with the thumb still in place. The bullion will automatically twist around to be anchored at the beginning of the back stitch. Repeat the bullions as many times as required. Take the needle down at the beginning of the back stitch.

Buttonhole Stitch and Blanket Stitch

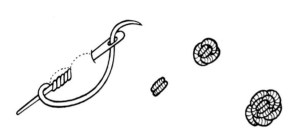

buttonhole stitch   *blanket stitch*

To make a buttonhole or blanket stitch, bring the needle up through the fabric, then take a short stitch, making sure to wind the thread under the needle, making a loop. You can work these stitches as long or as short as you wish. Buttonhole stitch is worked close together; blanket stitch is worked further apart.

Cretan Stitch

Cretan stitch is useful for creating a braided effect or textured leaves. It is worked with a centre line. Come out at the top of the line, take a stitch to the right of the line, then come out below and just to the right of the centre line. Now take a stitch to the left of the line, and come up just below the last stitch, and to the left of the centre line. Repeat in this manner till design is filled.

Chain Stitch

To make chain stitch, bring the needle up through the fabric and hold the thread down with the thumb of the left hand. Insert the needle into the same hole and make a small stitch, ensuring that the thread is placed under the needle to form a loop. Take the needle back down through the loop and repeat, securing the previous loop until you have reached the required length.

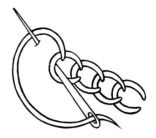

Colonial Knot

To make a colonial knot, bring the needle up through the fabric, hold the thread out from the fabric and place the needle under the thread, holding the needle to the right. Then wind the thread over the top of the needle from the left to the right. This will make a figure eight. Insert the needle back down through the fabric as close to the thread as possible. Hold the knot very firmly and close to the fabric with the thumb of your left hand, and then gently pull the thread through to the back.

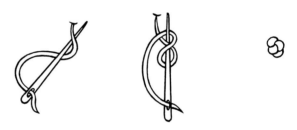

Coral Stitch

Coral stitch is very useful for stems and textured lines. It is also used as a fill-in stitch for which it is worked very close together. Stitched this way, it creates a great texture. Coral stitch is worked from right to left. Lay the thread along the line to be stitched, take a small stitch, place the thread over and then under the tip of the needle, then pull the thread through keeping the tension tight at all times.

Couching Stitch or Holding Stitch

Couching stitch is a straight stitch laid along the design and couched down with small slanted or straight stitches. This stitch can be used to couch a thread that is too thick or too fragile to use as a regular embroidery thread, or for making curves.

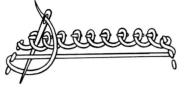

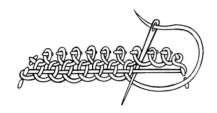

Detached Buttonhole Stitch and Blanket Stitch

Stem stitch or back stitch around the outline of the design that is to be filled with the detached buttonhole stitch. Work the detached buttonhole stitch from the left to the right, but do not pierce the fabric. Leave the stitches loose. Take the thread across the fabric from the right to the left, anchor the thread to the back stitch, or stem stitch, then repeat the buttonhole stitch by stitching into the loops of the previous row. Make sure that you include the laid thread in your buttonhole stitches. With some designs you may wish to leave an opening at the bottom of the design to stuff with toy fill. When filled, couch down the opening.

Feather Stitch

Bring the needle through to the front of the fabric. Hold the thread down with the thumb of the left hand, insert the needle a little to the right and down, and then take a small stitch, holding the thread under the needle. Hold the thread to the left side of the stitch and take a small stitch to the left and a little down. Repeat.

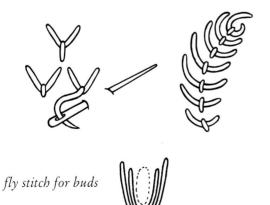

fly stitch for buds

Fly Stitch

Fly stitch is worked in the same way that a lazy daisy stitch is worked, except that you leave a space between where you bring the needle up and where you take the needle down, forming a 'Y' instead of a circle. Sometimes, when making a leaf, you cross over the first stitch, making one stitch longer than the other. By working the stitches close together and changing the length of them you can stitch a very nice leaf.

French Knot

To make a French knot, bring the needle up at the point where you want the knot, then wrap the thread around the needle once. Reinsert the needle as close as possible to where you came up. Hold the loop close and tight to the fabric with the thumb of your other hand as you pull the thread through to the back.

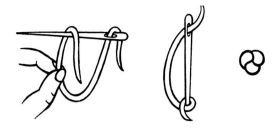

German Knotted Stitch Buttonhole

Work two buttonhole stitches close together, then pass the needle through the back of the last two stitches between the threads and the fabric. Pull gently to create a knot, then repeat the last three steps, leaving a gap between the knotted stitches. You can work this stitch back to back to make an interesting filling stitch.

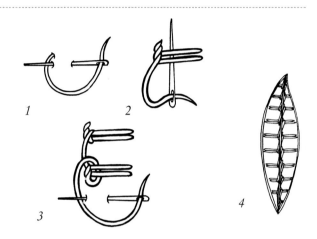

Granitos Stitch

Granitos stitch is created by coming up and going down in the same holes in the fabric. Bring the thread up to the front of the fabric, then go down a small distance from the entry point. Come out in the entry hole, lay the thread to the right of the first stitch, and go down in the same exit hole. Come up again in the same entry hole and lay the thread to the left of the centre stitch, then go down in the same exit hole. Repeat the centre stitch to create a nice rounded stitch. If you want the stitch to have more height, repeat all the stitches till you have the required shape.

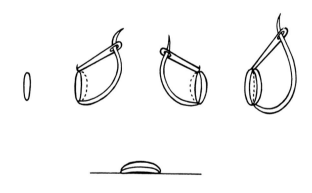

Herringbone Stitch

This is a great stitch to create pattern and texture. Bring the needle up through the fabric at the lower edge of the design, then take a small stitch by going in at the right and coming out on the left at the top of the design. Repeat this step again at the bottom and again at the top. This will give you a crossed over stitch at the top and bottom. The stitch lies on the top of the fabric.

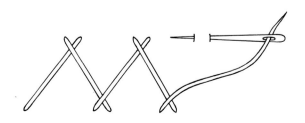

Lazy Daisy Stitch

This stitch is also called 'detached chain stitch'. Take a small stitch from the inside of a flower or the inside edge of a leaf. Where the needle has emerged, bring the thread around the needle tip to form a loop, then fasten with a short or long stitch, depending on the look you are after.

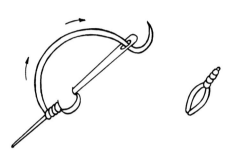

Lazy Daisy Bullion Stitch

Take a small stitch from the inside of a flower or the inside edge of a leaf. Where the needle has emerged, bring the thread around the needle tip to form a loop, then wrap the thread around the needle tip 3–5 times. Hold the stitch in place with your thumb, then pull the thread firmly. Fasten off by taking the thread through to the back of the fabric.

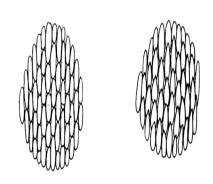

Needle Painting

Needle painting is used to cover the fabric, leaving no background showing through. It can be stitched in two ways: by stitching split stitch very closely together or by stitching long and short straight stitches that interlock together. The stitches are best if worked in an uneven manner so that ridges don't form. I would suggest that you practise on a separate piece of fabric until you find the method that suits you best.

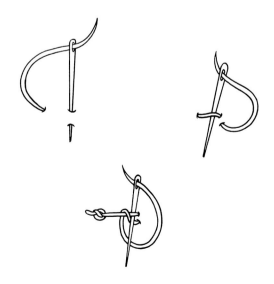

Palestrina Stitch or Double Knot Stitch

This stitch is a nice border stitch as it has quite a raised knot. Work the stitch from left to right by making a small straight stitch. Come back up and loop the needle and thread around and under the straight stitch. Pull through gently, keeping the thread rather loose. Place the needle back under the straight stitch again, still keeping the thread loose. Keep the thread under the needle, pull through and then tight to make a knot. Continue working in this manner, making the knots close together or further apart, depending on the look you are after.

Pistil Stitch

Bring the needle up through the fabric, holding the fabric firmly with the left hand. Twist the thread from under the needle over the top of the needle, from left to right, and then insert the needle back into the fabric a short distance from where the needle came out. Hold the thread firmly with the left thumb. This will make a straight stitch with a knot on the end.

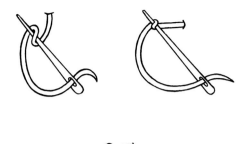

Ribbon Stitch

Bring the ribbon to the top of the fabric. Lay the ribbon flat on top of the fabric, then pierce the ribbon with the needle and pull the ribbon through to the back of the fabric, being careful not to pull the ribbon all the way through. This way you should leave a small curl at the tip of the leaf or petal.

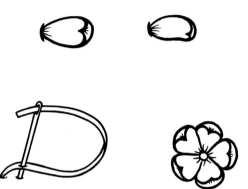

Rope Stitch

Rope stitch is like twisted chain stitch, but stitched much closer together. Bring the needle up through the fabric, insert the needle back into the fabric to the left of where the needle came up, pick up a small piece of fabric, and then wrap the thread under and around the needle and pull through. Insert the needle back into the fabric half-way down and to the left of the last stitch, pick up a small piece of fabric, then wrap the thread around and under the needle and pull through. Repeat the above steps and your stitch should look like a rope.

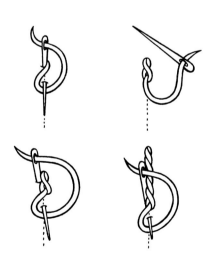

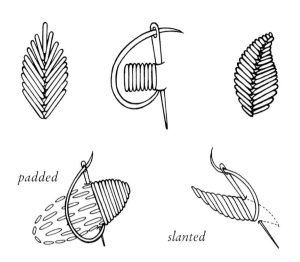

padded

slanted

Satin Stitch, Padded Satin Stitch and Slanted Satin Stitch

Satin stitch is straight stitches worked very close together to fill in a design. The stitches may be worked straight up and down or on a slant to give a different effect. First stitch around the design in split stitch or stem stitch, then fill in the shape with satin stitch, making sure not to leave any of the outline stitch showing.

Padded satin stitch is worked by outlining the shape in split stitch, filling the shape in with straight stitch or any other filling stitch, and then working the satin stitch over this to give a padded shape.

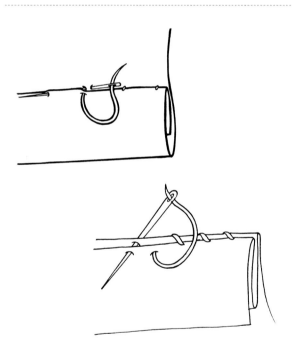

Slip Stitch and Over Sewing

Place the two edges of the fabric together and tack. Work from the right to the left by picking up small sections of the fabric at a time, pulling the thread through, and then picking up the next section, keeping your stitches even. This stitch is used to hold two pieces of fabric together and is very strong.

With slip stitch the needle is run under the fabric and a short over-sew stitch is used to pull the two pieces of fabric together.
The long stitch is run on the inside of the fabric where it won't be seen, and only a small amount of fabric is picked up on the surface.

Split Stitch

Split stitch is like stem stitch. It is worked the same way, but you bring the needle up through the last stitch, splitting the thread, instead of beside it. This is a good stitch for outlining a design for satin stitch or needle painting.

Stem Stitch

To work stem stitch you always keep the thread under the needle and work from left to right. Take even and regular stitches by bringing the needle out to the left half-way along the previous stitch. The stitches overlap each other to make a line or curve. Stem stitch may be used for outline, filling, stems and so on.

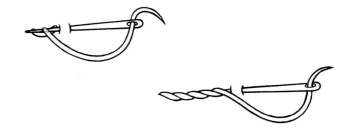

Straight Stitch

Straight stitch is worked at various intervals in short or long stitches. The stitch is laid across the fabric by coming up where you want the stitch to start and going down where you want the stitch to finish. Straight stitch is used for various aspects of a design, for example, stems, daisies and highlights.

Surface Stem Stitch

Surface stem stitch is a stem stitch, worked through a straight stitch and laid on the surface of the work. Start the stem stitch at the bottom of the design and always work it with the thread under the needle. Keep an even tension the whole time. A tapestry needle is used for this stitch.

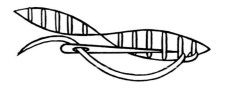

Tacking Stitch or Running Stitch

Tacking stitch is when the needle picks up an even amount of fabric on the front and back of the fabric in a line. Uses of tacking stitch are to hold two pieces of fabric together or for marking stitching lines.

Trellis Stitch

Trellis stitch is long straight stitches running vertically and horizontally (or diagonally). I weave the straight stitches under and over each other to anchor the thread. The intersections are secured with a small slanting stitch or a small cross stitch. Make sure the stitches are all facing in the same direction. This stitch is wonderful for filling in large areas.

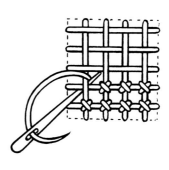

Turkey Stitch

This is like a back stitch, with one stitch pulled tight and the next stitch left loose. Bring the needle out on the left, then take a small stitch to the right and come out between the two. Repeat this stitch, pulling one stitch tight and leaving a loop in the next.

Whipped Back Stitch

Complete the back stitch in the usual manner, and then whip the thread under and over each back stitch, without going through the fabric. When whipping, it is better to use a tapestry needle — you can use the blunt end or eye of the needle to avoid splitting the surface thread.

Whipped Chain Stitch

Stitch a row of chain stitches, then with the other end of the needle or a tapestry needle, whip under each chain stitch without going through the fabric.

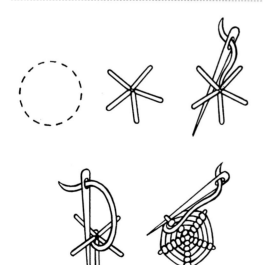

Whipped Spider Stitch

Draw a circle of the appropriate size, then stitch 5 or more straight stitches radiating out from the centre of the circle. Bring the needle up at the centre of the circle and slide the needle under 2 radiating stitches. Bring the needle back over and under the second thread and under the next thread. Proceed in this manner until all the radiating stitches are covered.

Whipped Stem Stitch

Stitch a row of stem stitch, then with the blunt end of the needle or a tapestry needle, whip under each stem stitch without going through the fabric.

Wool Rose Stitch

Work 5 to 6 satin stitches in the darkest shade to make a square. Work a second row of satin stitches across the first square to give a padded look. With the next shade of wool, bring the needle up half-way along the base of the square and down at a point two-thirds from the base on the right-hand side of the square. Then work 3 more stitches alongside, making sure that the needle always enters the fabric slightly higher than the last stitch, until the final stitch is the same height as the padded square. Rotate the work anti-clockwise and repeat 3 more times.

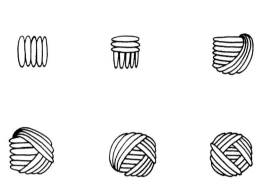

Woven Spider Rose Stitch

To make a spider rose, stitch a 5-spoke circle with a thread to match the rose. Thread the ribbon or thread onto a tapestry needle and weave the ribbon or thread under and over the spokes until you have the desired shape and fullness. The ribbon should be allowed to twist throughout this stitch to give the shape of rose petals.

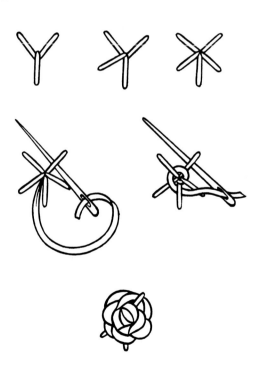

Materials and Techniques

All instructions are presented in good faith.

Needles

The size and type of the needle you use is mostly a personal choice. In general you will find that you graduate to a smaller needle the more confident you become. Keep in mind that you need to create a hole large enough to pull the thread or ribbon through so as not to damage it.

CREWEL

A fine needle with a medium-sized eye used for most forms of embroidery and heirloom. The lower the number of the needle, the thicker the thread you can use. The higher the number (No. 12 is the highest), the finer the thread and the finer the fabric you can use.

CHENILLE

A large, thick needle, with a large eye and sharp tip, used for silk ribbon and wool embroidery. The lower the number, the thicker the needle; the higher the number, the finer the needle.

STRAW

A long, sharp needle with a very small eye used for bullion stitch. The lower the number, the larger the needle and the thicker the thread you can use. The higher the number, the smaller the needle and the finer the thread you can use.

TAPESTRY

A thick, blunt needle that you can use for tapestry and spider roses, and also as a tool in loop stitch. The lower the number, the thicker the needle. The higher the number, the finer the needle.

Threads

When cutting thread, cut it no longer than the measurement from your wrist to your elbow (45cm [17 $^{1}/_{2}$"]). This stops the thread becoming distressed and tangled due to too much use. The thread will break down because of the number of times you pull it through the fabric; it will also lose its sheen. Always separate your stranded threads and then put them back together, as this makes the thread pass through the fabric more easily. No threads are guaranteed 100 per cent colourfast nowadays, so you will have to take care that the threads don't bleed into your fabric when you wash the embroidered piece. You may like to test the darker threads by wetting them and placing them onto a scrap of fabric: if the colour runs, you will have to rinse the thread until the water runs clear.

Silk Ribbons

Silk ribbon is used in much the same way as regular embroidery threads. Always use short lengths of ribbon, no longer than 25cm to 30cm (9 $^{3}/_{4}$" to 11 $^{3}/_{4}$"). To thread the ribbon onto the needle, pass the ribbon through the eye of the needle, then pass the point of the needle through the end of the ribbon to secure. Always treat ribbon with care and be gentle with it, and keep the ribbon loose, as this creates beauty in silk ribbon embroidery. The soft look is achieved with a gentle touch.

Hoops

I like to use a hoop at all times as I find I get a better finish and have more control over the embroidery. For this reason I would strongly recommend persevering with a hoop. Do not leave your embroidery in the hoop when you are not working on it, even while you make a cup of tea or coffee, as prolonged exposure in the hoop can damage your fabric. Cover the inside ring of your hoop with cotton tape to protect the fabric from damage. In time, you will need to have a hoop in all the different sizes for working with different stitches. I recommend the better quality hoops as the cheap ones are very rough and not very strong. The size of the hoop you use very much depends on what you can manage.

Transferring designs

I mostly use a water-soluble pen to mark my designs onto the fabric. If you use a water-soluble pen, wash and rinse your embroidery thoroughly after use. This will neutralise the chemical used in the pen and remove any excess pen marks from the fabric. For some designs, such as shadow work, you can use a HB pencil. This will give you a thinner line. Pencil is a little harder to remove from some fabrics so use with care. When marking the design onto fabric, mark only the minimum amount of the design necessary to stitch your embroidery so as to avoid unsightly marks on the fabric. It is always advisable to test a small amount of the fabric with whatever method you choose to see if they are compatible. I have started to experiment with water-soluble Vilene and have found it to be very successful to use with dark fabrics that are impossible to transfer your design onto. The Vilene needs to be rinsed out very thoroughly, as it is very sticky when wet.

To transfer your design to fabric, fold the fabric in half vertically and horizontally, and then finger press to find the centre of the fabric. Place the pattern under the fabric and line up with the centre folds. Pin the fabric and pattern together. Trace the pattern onto the fabric with a water-soluble pen or HB pencil. If you are unable to see the pattern through the fabric, hold it up to a window or use a light box to trace the pattern onto the fabric. When working with wool, transfer your design onto a separate piece of tracing paper. Place the design onto the wool and pin in place. Make holes in the pattern sheet where you wish to make a mark with your pen or pencil. It is advisable when transferring the design to mark and work one section of the flowers or design at a time, as it is very difficult to follow a multitude of marks on the fabric. Keep placing the design back on the fabric after completing a section of embroidery and mark the next section.

Magnification

Many embroiderers have trouble seeing the fine stitches in some embroidery projects. There are many sewing aids on the market with magnifiers in them; magnifying glasses, stands with magnifiers, magnifiers for around the neck and on the head are just a few. You will have to ask around and try different types to find the one that suits you best. Students and customers of mine who have found a magnifying aid that suited them say that these have made their embroidery more enjoyable, as well as helping them to tackle pieces that they had found difficult. It is also very important to have a good light source to work under: lamp, window or daylight. There are many very good lamps on the market for you to choose from; you just have to find the one that suits you best.

Comfort When Stitching

It is very important to have a comfortable, firm chair to sit on when stitching. If you find that you are getting a sore neck, place your feet on a raised surface — a covered brick will do — as this straightens your posture to a more upright position. If you find that you are still leaning forward too much, place a very firmly packed cushion on your lap, which will make you hold your embroidery up, and in turn you will straighten your back and lift up your head, taking the pressure off your neck.

Getting Started

Wash your hands before you start any embroidery. You may use a knot to start if the back of your work won't be seen. Start with a knot or a small over-sew stitch and finish in the same manner. If you can see the back of the work, stitch a tiny over-sew stitch where it will be under some embroidery, leaving a long tail so that you can go back later and thread the ends through the back of your work.

Washing

Always wash your embroidery with good quality soap and rinse thoroughly. Finish with a final rinse in distilled water. Dry on a towel out of the sun. Place the embroidery face down on a clean soft towel to iron.

Construction of Finished Blankets

These instructions are for referral when making the May Bear's Baby Blanket, Honey 'B' Bears Blanket, Coming Ready-or-not Blanket, Morning Stroll Blanket and the Heart's Desire Baby Blanket

Cut your backing fabric 1.3m x 1m (50 ^{3}/4" x 39"). This will leave a 10cm (4") overhang on all sides of your blanket when the two are pinned together. Pin the piping 5cm (2") from the edge of the blanket, raw edges to the outside. Cut and overlap the corners, and pin and stitch in place using a zipper foot (Fig. 1). Place the backing fabric face down on a table, then place the embroidered blanket right side up on top and pin in place.

Fold the corners over, the same way you would if you were covering a book, at a 45° angle (Fig. 2). Fold the sides over and turn under 5cm (2"), then turn over again so that you have a 5cm (2") double thickness border on the front of the blanket. Pin in place. Trim away any material showing at the corners so that there is a mitred edge. Hand-stitch the backing in place (Fig. 3).

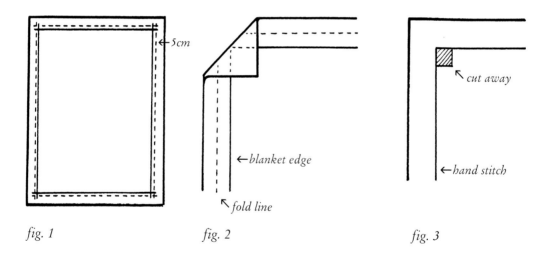

fig. 1   fig. 2   fig. 3

Enlargement Guide

Some older photocopiers enlarge to a maximum of only 141%.
To enlarge the illustrations and templates if this is the case, follow these instructions.

To enlarge to:	Photocopy enlargement percentage	
200%	first x 141%	then x 141%
150%	first x 141%	then x 106%

Stockists

When ringing Australia from overseas take the 0 out at the front of the first number and put 61 in instead.

Dinky Dye Threads
Distributer: Jo Fisher/Mason
84 Tibradden Circle
Ascot WA 6104 Australia
Phone: 08 9479 7918
Email: jo@dinkydye.com
Website: www.dinkydyes.com

Caron Threads; Waterlilies & Watercolours
Kindred Spirits Designs
Ben Britim Distributors
Scarlett Street
Mittagong NSW 2575 Australia
Phone: 02 4871 2415
Fax: 02 4872 2663
Email: benbri@bigpond.net.au

DMC Stranded Cotton and Perle Cotton
Distributer: Radda Australia
PO Box 317
Earlwood NSW 2206 Australia
Phone: 02 9559 3088
Fax: 02 9558 5204
Email: cservice@radda.com.au
Website: www.dmc.com

Distributer: Gumnut Yarns
PO Box 519
Mudgee NSW 2850 Australia
Phone: 02 6374 2661
Fax: 02 6374 2771
Email: sales@gumnutyarns.com
Website: www.gumnutyarns.com

Kindred Spirits
Embroidery Designs
Distributer: Gail Rogers
11 Riversea View
Mosman Park WA 6012 Australia
Phone: 08 9384 8758
Fax: 08 9384 8758
Email: gail@kindredspirits.com.au
Website: www.kindredspirits.com.au

YLI Silk Ribbon and Cotton Laces
Distributer: Cotton on Creations
PO Box 318
Blackheath NSW 2785 Australia
Phone: 02 4787 6588
Fax: 02 4787 6544
Email: cottoncreations@bigpond.com.au
Website: www.cottononcreations.com.au

Cotton Laces
Distributor: Heirloom Essentials
PO Box 578
Epping NSW 1710 Australia
Phone: 02 9876 5484
Fax: 02 9876 8015
Email: heirloomlace@bigpond.com.au

The Thread Gatherer Threads (Sheep's Silk),
Silken Ribbons, Caron Threads, Waterlilies &
Watercolours, Mill Hill Beads
Distributor: Ireland Needlecraft
PO Box 1175
Narre Warren VIC 3805 Australia
Phone: 03 9702 3222
Fax: 03 9702 3255
Email: enquries@irelandneedlecraft.com.au
Website: www.irelandneedlecraft.com.au

Colour Streams Silk Ribbon and Silk Threads
Distributor: Colour Streams
5 Palm Avenue
Mullumbimby NSW 2482 Australia
Phone/Fax: 02 6684 2577
Email: colourstreams@colourstreams.com.au
Website: www.colourstreams.com.au

Wool Blanketing and Wool Flannel
Geelong Blanket Company
143 Church Street
Geelong West VIC 3218 Australia
Phone: 03 5277 2006
Fax: 03 5277 1925
Email: geelblan@iprimus.com.au

Water-soluble Vilene 541,
German Beech Hoops, Piping, Pellon
Distributor: Birch Haberdashery & Craft
PO Box 5060 MDC
Heidelberg West VIC 3081 Australia
Phone: 03 9450 8900
Fax: 03 9450 8999
Email: orders@birchhaby.com.au
Website: www.birchhaby.com.au

About the Author

It is exciting to have the opportunity to share with you the excitement and joy I have had in designing and sewing new pieces for this book.

I am not sure when my pastime turned into an obsession, but after working and designing in the needlework industry, having several articles in print and writing my second book I wonder where the time has gone. To have my first book, Creative Ribbons & Roses, translated into Spanish for a Mexican publisher was beyond my wildest dreams. (The English version is available in reprint from Sally Milner Publishing.) I hope you enjoy this new book even more.

Experience from my studio/outlet, Kindred Spirits, in Mosman Park, Western Australia, exposed me to the full range of threads and materials that are available. This enabled me to select from the best in the world for embellishing my creations. However, I have now retired from the shop in order to concentrate exclusively on designing new patterns to add to the Kindred Spirits range.

One of my greatest pleasures is working directly with students. While they learn from me, I learn from them, constantly clarifying and redeveloping pattern presentation. Their interests and requests constantly stimulate the design process.
With the work of my wonderful graphic artist, Nicole Moffat, I am confident that the designs will be easy to follow at home without the assistance of a teacher.

As a child growing up on an isolated wheat and sheep farm in the wheat belt of Western Australia, I learnt to be self-sufficient, and spent many a happy hour wandering about the property with the dog and cat in tow. This time spent amusing myself from a very early age allowed me space to be creative. This, I think, has been the grounding for a lifetime of creative pursuits. Now, living in suburban Perth, I appreciate that even in a city specialist help can sometimes be difficult to access.

For the last seven years I have been developing and producing embroidery designs for Kindred Spirits, as well as teaching. I am constantly excited about creating new embroidery designs in all mediums. Every day some new idea develops and takes shape, waiting for me to have the time to stitch it. The only problem is: where is the time? I'm passionate about anything to do with the creative medium and my life has been a constant struggle to fit in all the exciting things there are to do.

Our house, walls and garage are repositories for the skeletons and workings of passions, past and present, and stores squirrelled away for the future. There are the obvious materials and threads (of every description) for embroidery, heirloom sewing, smocking, cross stitch, tapestry, quilting and patchwork. Add the essentials for screen printing, pottery, sculpture, painting, printmaking, teddy bears and stamping, and you get the picture.

I'm married and have three adult children. John and I live with two crazy pomeranian puppies and a more sedate elderly papillon who shadows my every move.

With all things in life, it is not the destination that is important but the journey, with all its twists and turns.

Gail Rogers